THOSE I HAVE KNOWN

THOSE I HAVE KNOWN

Anwar el-Sadat

JONATHAN CAPE
THIRTY BEDFORD SQUARE LONDON

First published in Great Britain 1985
Copyright © 1984 by Mayo National Publishing House, Cairo, Egypt

Jonathan Cape Ltd, 30 Bedford Square, London WC1B 3EL

British Library Cataloguing in Publication Data
Sadat, Anwar el-
Those I have known.
1. Near East – Politics and government
– 1945 –
I. Title
956'.04'0924   DS63
ISBN 0-224-02983-5

Printed in Great Britain by
Ebenezer Baylis & Son Ltd
The Trinity Press, Worcester and London

CONTENTS

Introduction 1

1 · The Birth of the Revolution 3
2 · Encounters with the Shah 16
3 · My Views of Khomeini 35
4 · Conflict with Colonel Qadaffi 42
5 · The Rancor of Nikita Khrushchev 51
6 · King Faisal, a Man of Dignity 63
7 · My Love for Gamal Abdel Nasser 73
8 · Nasser's Death and My Relations with Tito 84
9 · My Peace Initiative 97
10 · Egypt and the Arabs 108
11 · Israel's Hostile Actions 114
12 · My Relations with Britain 121
13 · Memories of War 130

INTRODUCTION

The dates of May 15 and October 6 stand out as landmarks in the life of Anwar el-Sadat. For Sadat, October 6 was his day of victory and honor, the day he took office as the third elected president of Egypt. It also revived sad memories for him, for on that day in 1973 he lost his younger brother, an air force pilot who took part, under the command of Husni Mubarak, at that time commander of the Egyptian air force, in the aerial attack that led to the recapture of the east bank of the Suez Canal by the Egyptian army.

Sadat saw October 6 as the day on which he achieved victory for Egypt after a series of defeats at the hands of the Israelis. The Egyptian soldier thus regained confidence, and the Egyptian people regained confidence in Sadat's leadership and in the army. Sadat always believed that if it had not been for the action of October 6 there would have been no subsequent peace. The state of no war–no peace that followed the defeat of June 5, 1967, led to complete paralysis in Egypt and throughout the Arab world. This is why when Sadat thought of offering a contribution to the Egyptian press he launched the magazine known today as *October*.

When Sadat created his own party, the National Democratic party, two years after his historic trip to Jerusalem, he started planning a party newspaper and at once thought of another important date in his career: May 15, 1971, when he overcame his political opponents and started his process of internal liberalization.

It took Sadat one year, thinking and contemplating, talking to many people and asking for new ideas and advice, for this was his style whenever he undertook an important task. Finally, he was satisfied with the quality and design of the paper he planned, which was to be called *Mayo* to commemorate his May 15 anniversary.

In December 1980, he held his first meeting with Abdallah Abdel Bari, chairman of the new publication, and Ibrahim Saada, the editor in chief. It was decided at that meeting that the president would write a historical narration for the paper, connecting the prerevolutionary period and the post–1952 period with today.

After considering the idea, Sadat said it was almost impossible for him to write the complete story, for that was the job of a professional historian. But suddenly his eyes sparkled, and to those who knew him it meant he had found a solution. Sadat said he would devote one page a week to writing about different personalities, politicians, heads of state, in Egypt, the Arab world, and world-wide. The president said this would provide a good opportunity for the youth of Egypt to learn something of their recent history, for those who had no past would have no future.

The president said he had stopped his journalistic writing nine or ten years ago, and it would be difficult to resume. He then suggested that a tape recorder should be used in weekly sessions with him. The recording and writing sessions began early in 1981 and went on every week until October 6, 1981, when he was assassinated. Some were published in *Mayo* at the time, others were written or recorded for later use. Those assembled here, for the first time, represent fragments of an unfinished life story.

· 1 ·

THE BIRTH OF THE REVOLUTION

When the July revolution broke out in 1952 we considered the old warrior, Aziz al-Masri, its uncontested godfather. This is why when we differed about handling the issue of the king we went to him for advice. Those days that shook Egypt started with our decision in January 1952 to carry out the revolution in three years' time. The founding committee of the Free Officers' movement met in the home of Hassan Ibrahim in Heliopolis and decided to plan for the revolution to take place during November 1955.

It appeared to us that we needed this time in order to complete the Free Officers' Association, so that it could carry out its responsibilities to the revolution. Though the base for the Free Officers' movement was there in 1952, we thought the "moment" was not yet ripe.

We chose the month of November because during that month the king returned from his annual summer vacation in Alexandria. We did not want to carry out our revolution in the summer, which would mean our forces would have to be split between Cairo and Alexandria. We wanted to strike at one place and at one time. After making that decision we went back to the barracks. Abdel Hakim Amer, Salah Salem, and myself served at Rafah, while Gamal Salem served at al-Arish, and Gamal Abdel Nasser in Cairo.

Soon after we had made our decision, Cairo was in flames caused by rioting, and Gamal Abdel Nasser felt that the fire provided an opportunity to begin the revolution immediately. The capital was under curfew with the army the only force in control. So we reasoned, what if the army (it was in the center of the capital) announced it was taking over governmental authority? It was an appealing question, but the situation was not that simple. The important thing was not the strength of the forces in Cairo but the number of those who were loyal to us. Our estimates were that upon the outbreak of the revolution we would have no more than one battalion on our side. Gamal Abdel Nasser went around the city to find those who were loyal to us, and he tried to meet some officers in a camp in the center of Cairo; but he found the situation was not encouraging, so we postponed the date. This time, however, it was not postponed to November 1955, as we had previously decided, but to November 1952. We thus brought the timing of the revolution forward three years. One of the reasons for this was that according to information which I had conveyed to Nasser, the king's reign was over and he was thinking of leaving the country.

Yousuf Rashad, the confidant of King Farouk, had informed me that after the fire in Cairo in January the king was preparing to leave. He had chosen the people to accompany him, ten in all, among them Yousuf Rashad himself. The king had not informed anyone of his planned departure except Rashad, whom he trusted deeply, and Rashad had passed on to me this grave secret. During one of my holidays I told Nasser: "The king is completely broken and is thinking of escaping." Then I related to Nasser the secret that Rashad had told me.

This is why the timing was advanced first to November 1952 and then to July of the same year.

The political developments that had taken place from January to July 1952 also led to our conviction that the time was ripe. During that period four cabinets were formed. And on the twentieth of July Naguib el-Hilaili was asked to form his second cabinet for six months. This cabinet lasted only a few hours, after which the revolution took place. While the cabinet was being formed, we were informed that Naguib el-Hilaili had chosen Hussein Sirry Amer for the post of minister of war. Nasser knew that his name had been sent to the king among the new nominees and that el-Hilaili had chosen him for that post to please the king. But what was more serious was the fact that Hussein Sirry knew seven of us personally, and he was quoted as having said: "I will show you who are the free officers."

Thus we expected that he would round up those of us he knew as soon as he took up his new cabinet post and so kill the revolution before its birth, or at least force us to postpone it for several years.

When Nasser was informed about these developments, he said: "If we wait Hussein Sirry will destroy us. We will have to eat him before he eats us." On the basis of this Nasser issued his orders to start the revolution. But what Nasser did not know at the time was that the king had omitted Hussein Sirry from his cabinet and chosen his brother-in-law, Ismail Shirin, for the post of minister of war. Ismail Shirin did not have a chance to exercise his authority for even one day.

Nasser sent Hassan Ibrahim to inform me about the decision at the al-Arish airport. On the evening of July 20 I received a telephone call asking me to be at the airport the next day, the twenty-first of July, because Hassan Ibrahim would be arriving from Cairo with a message from "Abou Menkar," which was the code name we had given to Nasser. As soon as we met he said, "Abou Menkar asks you to leave for Cairo tomorrow. The revolution has been set to take place between July 22 and August 15. It could happen any time during that period."

I left Hassan Ibrahim to inform Gamal Salem, who was also at the al-Arish airport, and went back to my unit commander to ask for a holiday. I told him my mother was very sick, and he granted me an immediate leave of absence.

Next day, the twenty-second of July, I took the military train from Rafah at eight o'clock in the morning and arrived in Cairo by four o'clock in the afternoon, but I couldn't find Nasser. In the past I used to find him waiting for me with his second-hand Austin whenever I came to Cairo, but this time he was not there. I went to my home and, as it was summer and I enjoy outdoor movies, I took my wife Jihan to the cinema.

When we returned to our home, I found a message from Nasser who had written to tell me that the project would take place that night and that we were to meet at Abdel Hakim's home at eleven o'clock. I asked the porter about the officer who left the message. He said: "The officer, your colleague, came twice, once at eight o'clock, and the other at ten o'clock. I told him you were at the cinema; I had no idea which one, so he left the card."

Later I learned that Nasser did not wait for me at the station because he was busy with the Free Officers preparing them for the night's operation. I had never imagined that the message I received would lead to them carrying out the revolution immediately upon my arrival in Cairo. I put on my uniform and hurried to the headquarters at Kubeh Bridge. By this time it was between twelve-thirty and one o'clock in the morning. I heard gunfire. The operation had begun, and our forces were clearing the area. An officer stopped me and prevented me from entering headquarters, as his orders were not to allow in any high-ranking officers. I tried to convince him that I belonged to the revolutionary group, but he would not listen; then I heard the voice of Abdel Hakim Amer telling them to release me and informing me that the operation had succeeded. We were in control of army headquarters. We walked to the headquarters, which is now the ministry of defense. The same place that had witnessed my interrogation was now the command post of the revolution. All of us spent the night there and stayed until the king left the country on July 26. Next morning I sat down to write the communiqué announcing the revolution, and broadcast it myself. Then we discussed the steps that were to follow.

The first step was to choose a prime minister. At the same time we wanted to enlarge our conflict with the king, but we wanted to carry out a careful and calculated plan so that our forces could arrive in Alexandria where Farouk spent the summer. We discussed the nominee for the post and decided upon Ali Maher. I was known to the public for my political activity; so Nasser asked me to meet with Ali Maher and request that he form a cabinet on behalf of the whole revolutionary council.

I did not know where Ali Maher's home was, since pashas at the time were a remote class. I called Ihsan Abdel Koddeus (a leading Egyptian journalist and novelist) and asked him if he knew where Ali Maher lived. He said that he did; so I asked him to accompany me. His home was at Giza where the Vietnamese embassy is located today.

Ali Maher received us on a small balcony on the second floor. I told him that I had come on behalf of the revolutionary council to ask him to form the new cabinet. As we were talking four planes passed over our heads, and he asked: "Are they with you?" I answered, "Yes, of course." He sighed and continued his conversation with me. Ihsan Abdel Koddeus was continually nudging me as the conversation progressed, and when Maher left us for a while, I asked Ihsan: "Why are you nudging me, is anything wrong?" He said: "Yes, the publisher Idgar Galad is in the next room and is eavesdropping, and you didn't notice." Galad was a king's man, and it appeared that Maher had asked him to listen in on the conversation in order to report it because Ali Maher wasn't yet ready to abandon the king. I told Ihsan: "Yes, I wanted Galad to overhear the conversation; this is why I was talking in a loud voice so that he will convey it to the king."

Ali Maher returned after a while and looked at me and said: "Truly, I would like to form a cabinet, but you know that for the past ten years I have had my problems with the king and Ahmed Hassanein, and also with the parties. I don't know whether you will continue on your path or not, or whether I will wake up one day and find you out of office. If that happens, then the king will cut off my head."

I then asked him: "Is this your final decision?"

He said: "Give me time to consult with the king and to reach an understanding with him."

I agreed.

I left Ali Maher and returned to headquarters, and after a while Ali Maher called back and said: "I have called the king and he agreed that I should form a new cabinet. I am scheduled to meet him at five." But before Ali Maher went to see the king in Alexandria he called us back and said that he would like to see us.

Both Nasser and I agreed to meet Ali Maher again at his home in Giza. But before we left we decided we should be ready to break openly with the king. We concluded that if we presented a number of unacceptable demands to him he would become emotional and reject them. That would then give us a pretext to open fire on his guards. So we carefully chose six demands, insignificant to us, but calculated to enrage him. The most important of these demands were the appointment of Muhammad Naguib as commander in chief of the army, and the removal of all the king's men from command positions.

Ali Maher received us at his home in a state of great satisfaction, thinking he had won both the king and the revolution over to his side. We presented our demands and were surprised to hear him reply: "I think the king will be quite receptive to your requests. From the telephone conversations I have had with him today, I have sensed his readiness to reach an understanding with you. He is unlikely to raise problems with the revolution; so hopefully this issue can be quickly resolved."

Ali Maher bade us farewell and left to see the king, who was waiting impatiently in Alexandria, admitting him to the palace without protocol. Shortly after I was surprised to receive an urgent phone call from Ali Maher in Alexandria. "What's happening?" I asked. He responded by saying that the king had agreed to all our demands. He had not only appointed Muhammad Naguib commander in chief of the army, he had also promoted him to the rank of general. I asked: "And his entourage? Are they excluded?"

"All your requests have been granted," said Ali Maher. "But I think that you and one of your colleagues should come to the palace to sign the visitors' book and thank the king for what he has done. By so doing we shall be able to solve any other problems, and everything will proceed smoothly."

"All right," I said. "I will answer you tomorrow."

I informed Gamal about the telephone call with Ali Maher on the night of July 24. I then allowed a day to pass without replying to Maher and he finally called me to ask why I had not turned up to sign the visitors' book. "I shall come today," I replied. "Meet me in the cabinet building in Alexandria." Meanwhile our revolutionary forces were moving toward Alexandria so that we would have a firm grip on the city when the time came. I had agreed with Gamal that I should go to Alexandria and present an ultimatum to the king as soon as our forces had complete control of the city, but not before. I would present the ultimatum and demand his abdication. But we could not do this until we were ready. Hence the delays.

It seems that some of my colleagues were jealous of the role I was playing and of my contacts with Ali Maher, but this was a quite natural role for me because of my previous political activity and because Maher knew no one else on the Revolutionary Council.

I spoke again with Nasser before leaving on my mission to Alexandria. I told him my analysis was that the king had been completely broken since the events of the Cairo fire—the evidence for this was the list he had prepared of people he would take abroad with him. There was going to be no problem with the king, I concluded. Faced with our ultimatum, he would abdicate and there would be no reason for us to waste our energy fighting a battle we were winning anyway. Gamal was satisfied with my analysis and said: "The important thing is to rid me of this headache over the king, then we will have control of the situation." I can see him to this day, thirty years later, standing there smoking a Craven A cigarette.

Then Muhammad Naguib came in and asked to accompany me to Alexandria. This had not been in our plans, but Gamal and I both welcomed him and we flew together in an air force plane from an old airport close to Nasser's home in Heliopolis. From the el-Nozha airport in Alexandria we went directly to the cabinet offices in Bolkly, where we were received by dozens of journalists and photographers. Naguib and I found Ali Maher waiting for us in his office with a worried frown on his face. "Why were you delayed?" he asked. "Is anything wrong?"

"No, nothing," I answered. He told me the king was worried because of our delay. He again asked us to sign the visitors' book, thanking the king for responding to our demands. Such a request obviously reflected the king's concern as well as Ali Maher's. They were unsure of our real intentions. But I had to keep them waiting a little longer until I was sure of our control over the city. So I said I would come and see them again at six o'clock, in three hours' time.

I went immediately to Camp Mostafa Pasha to see Zakaria Mohieddin, then chief of staff of the revolutionary council and responsible for the movement of our forces. He told me he could not be ready until eight o'clock the following morning because troops were still arriving and would need rest and food. He had to make sure he had control of all the palaces, or else the king might manage to flee from one palace to another. So once again I had to postpone my meeting with Ali Maher, which of course had only one real purpose: to deliver the ultimatum to the king.

When I told him I was postponing my visit until nine o'clock, his voice was full of concern. The king had been asking him about the troop movements in Alexandria. I tried to reassure him, saying it was simply to ensure the security of the country and of foreigners. Of course, he was thinking all this time of supporting the king while at the same time making sure he remained prime minister. My main concern was to ensure our military control so that I could present the ultimatum and bring the nightmare to an end.

We spent the night working at the camp, with Zakaria Mohieddin reviewing all the army postings so that the king could not escape. Gamal Salem arrived from Cairo. He had been in al-Arish when the revolution broke out and had been sent up to Alexandria by Nasser to help with the ultimatum.

My view all along had been that we should not involve ourselves in a battle if we were going to win our ends anyway. But Gamal Salem thought it would be best to kill the king. I said there was no need to kill him because he would flee the country the moment we presented the ultimatum. Our aim should be to keep control of the situation so that we could proceed with our work and achieve our goals. I told Salem that Nasser had agreed with me that there should be no unnecessary bloodshed. Once blood started to flow it might never stop. The discussion went on and on, with Naguib sitting between us as umpire and Mohieddin arranging the placement of his troops on a map. By two o'clock in the morning Gamal Salem said he was going to report back to Nasser and consult with him. We were not to make any moves until we heard from him further.

We continued writing out the ultimatum in longhand until it was finished. Then I folded the paper and went to bed.

Next day I headed out for Bolkly without waiting to hear from Gamal Salem, because I had agreed on everything beforehand with Nasser. Ali Maher had told the press we were on the way, and we found about two hundred journalists waiting for us. We entered Ali Maher's office and were given two chairs facing his desk. He seemed to be delighted because everything, he thought, was moving in the direction of his own interests and he figured that he would receive the blessings of both the king and the revolutionaries. He thought he was on the way to becoming the only center of power in the country, once he had gotten rid of the old political parties.

Maher was very content as he sat there and asked us to have coffee with him. He leaned back in his chair with confidence and said to us: "I hope you have come with your decision."

"Yes, of course," I replied. I reached for my briefcase and got out the written ultimatum, moved to his desk and read it out in a loud voice. Then I dropped it into his hands. I saw him shrinking in his chair as a minute passed, seeming like a century. He took a breath and then said to us with difficulty: "Are you confident you will succeed?"

"Of course," I said. "Good for the king and Ahmed Hassanein," he answered. "They deserve it."

Then Maher began to narrate to us stories of corruption in the palace. When he had finished, he looked up at me and said: "Farouk thought the end had come on July twenty-third. He said this would not end calmly and I tried to comfort him. But he was right." He then told us the king had become very concerned that morning when troops encircled the Ras al-Tin Palace at seven o'clock and skirmishes had broken out between the royal guards and the revolutionary forces. But the king had ordered his men to cease fire and close the palace gates. He was terrified that the guards were about to slay him and called on the American ambassador to protect him.

After Ali Maher had finished his story about the king's reactions, I asked him to deliver the ultimatum to the king, saying that if he did not leave the country by six o'clock that same night we would not be responsible for the consequences. Ali Maher stood up to receive the ultimatum, and I asked him to sign a receipt for it. Then I called Mohieddin to escort him to the palace. The meeting with the king did not take him five minutes. Soon he was calling me again from Bolkly, the cabinet office, to say: "Congratulations. The king has accepted the ultimatum and will leave the country by six o'clock." We then met with Soliman Hafez, the cabinet's legal adviser, to draw up the abdication formula, and Hafez took it to the king for his signature. The king's hands were shaking so much Hafez had to ask him to sign it twice.

My task was to start preparations for the departure of the king's yacht, the *Mahroussa*, which took six hours to get ready to sail. I then ordered the air force and the coast guard to salute the king as he was leaving. I had received notice that the coast guard was preparing to fire on the royal yacht, and I wanted to be certain that the operation ended without bloodshed. The hour that divided two eras came. At 6:00 P.M. on July 26, 1952, Muhammad Naguib, Hussein el-Shafei, later a vice-president, and Gamal Salem all boarded the royal yacht to pay farewell to the king while I stayed on board the command destroyer *Ibrahim*. The historic moment passed peacefully, with no bloodshed as Nasser and I had desired.

But Gamal Abdel Nasser had in the meantime had another session with Gamal Salem in Cairo. Salem had told him about our disagreement over how to handle the king and woke him at three in the morning to say the king had to be killed. Nasser told him to go and see Aziz al-Masri, who would judge who was right and who was wrong. They both went around to al-Masri's house and woke him up to tell him of our disagreement about the fate of the king: Salem wanted him executed; Sadat wanted him to abdicate and leave the country peacefully.

Al-Masri was a revolutionary who believed in the use of force. So he told them they should not leave the king alive; he must be slain. But Nasser decided in the end not to follow al-Masri's advice, although we considered him our tutor and—as I have said—the godfather of our revolution. During his final years, we wanted to give him his due, and when he asked to go as ambassador to Moscow, where he had many friends, we allowed him to do so.

After his retirement al-Masri lived peacefully at his apartment in Zamalek until his death. All of us marched in his funeral parade and afterward boarded a helicopter to Borg el-Arab, which after our long service in the desert was closest to our hearts and where we always liked to go for contemplation and relaxation.

There I sat, surrounded by all the solitude, liberating my soul and thoughts. I said words that nobody heard: "God bless his soul, the fighter who never gave up. God bless the soul of the man who prepared the way for our revolution. May the soul of Aziz al-Masri rest in peace."

·2·

ENCOUNTERS WITH THE SHAH

Born in 1918 in the depths of the countryside, I was raised in that gentle land to which I became attached. My dream at that time was to grow up, join the Military College, and graduate as an officer in the Egyptian army. That dream came true. In 1938, I graduated as an officer with the rank of second lieutenant.

I recall this today as I take up my pen to write about the Shah of Iran. It was a strange coincidence that brought us together. He was also born in 1918 and graduated from the Military College in 1938—and with the same rank. But there the comparisons between the shah and myself ended.

I came from a family of peasants in the little Egyptian village of Mit Abul-Kom; he was the son of an emperor and the successor to the throne of an old and mighty empire. My dreams went no further than gradual advancement in the military corps, serving in the Egyptian army until I retired, when I would return once again to the land I loved. As for the shah, a great future awaited him. His dreams were limitless. His father the emperor, who was known for his severity and determination, was training him to take over on his death. The emperor paid great attention to his son's education and, wishing him to learn the art of warfare, sent him to a military college like any other student.

At that time, and under those circumstances, I never imagined that I would one day make the acquaintance of the Shah of Iran. The very year we graduated, however, Ali Maher, the Egyptian prime minister, persuaded King Fouad to arrange a political marriage. He proposed that the heir to the throne of Iran should marry the Egyptian king's daughter, Princess Fawzia. The shah was head of a Shiite Islamic state; King Fouad, the head of a Sunni Islamic state. The marriage, as Ali Maher saw it, would draw the two countries together, unite their interests and put an end to their differences.

The Persians had created an empire and civilization before the appearance of Islam or even the birth of the Arabic language. Persian civilization spread to all parts of the world, and today there are still those in the East, especially in Pakistan and India, who speak Persian as the language of civilization and culture (and after the 1952 revolution I decided to learn Persian, too).

The marriage between the man who was to become shah and the king of Egypt's daughter was duly agreed upon. Preparations for the wedding began. And here I leap ahead to the year 1971. On October 11 of that year I was on my way to pay an official visit to the Soviet Union and was received by the shah during a stopover at the airport in Teheran. I had previously had a meeting with him at the Islamic summit in Rabat in 1969, following the burning of the al-Aqsa mosque.

Recalling that meeting, I put a question to the shah as soon as we began to speak. "How many times have our paths crossed?" I asked. Greatly surprised at the question, he replied: "This is the second time we have met. Our first meeting was in Rabat."

"No," I said. "It is the third time! Perhaps you will not remember our first encounter."

"And when was that?" he asked in astonishment.

"In 1938," I answered. "That year we both graduated as second lieutenants. You came to Cairo as heir to the throne of Iran to marry King Fouad's daughter. A military parade was held in the desert at Alamaza. I was in the Fourth Battalion, Infantry Rifles. You sat with Prince Farouk to watch the military parade I participated in."

I went on: "You were on a raised platform and I passed before you in the parade. The distance between us was very small, yet in reality it was great. For you were the heir to the throne and I was a mere officer from an Egyptian village you have never heard of." We both laughed.

Then I said to the shah: "We have an Arabic saying: 'There can be no love except after enmity.' The friendship that follows upon enmity is, in fact, stronger and more durable. You will recall the fight we had in Rabat before the heads of state of the Islamic world. There is indeed truth in the Arabic saying, for we quarreled and now are friends." Our quarrel had been a bitter one, but our friendship grew steadily over the years and was to stand us both in good stead.

The quarrel in Rabat happened at the Islamic summit meeting of 1969. I had gone to the meeting as head of the Egyptian delegation, and President Nasser had asked me to take advantage of my presence there to meet the shah and attempt to settle the differences that existed between our two countries. Nasser had suggested I ask King Hussein of Jordan, who was also present at the summit, to intercede with the shah and arrange a meeting. Nasser himself had been unable to attend the meeting because he had suffered a severe heart attack. King Hussein gladly agreed to our request, and we decided I would meet the shah at King Hussein's residence.

I had had a long day of visits with the heads of Islamic states, who had come to Morocco to decide what to do after the burning of the al-Aqsa mosque by arsonists in Jerusalem . . . how to protect the Muslim holy places that had fallen under Israeli control. It looked like it was going to be a difficult meeting, for the heads of state feared that I had been sent to bring about the failure of the meeting. I said to them: "It is not true that I have come to sabotage the conference. We are all here to examine the situation following the burning of al-Aqsa mosque. It is essential, in these circumstances, that we all work together to make a success of this conference. So have no fear."

They had been reassured. King Faisal of Saudi Arabia told the other heads of state he was well acquainted with Anwar el-Sadat. He was not the sort of man, he told them, who would deliberately sabotage a conference of such significance to Muslims everywhere. My position as head of the Egyptian delegation was not without its difficulties, either. My enemies had been infuriated when Nasser chose me to take his place as head of the delegation during his illness. They had imagined Ali Sabri, the former prime minister and Nasser's second in command, to be their leader. Great had been the blow, therefore, when Nasser chose me instead. There was little they could do about this, although they had persuaded Nasser to include one of their men in the Rabat delegation, Labib Shukair, at that time speaker of the People's Assembly. Shukair's job was to spy on me. I had raised no objections, although I was quite aware of their aims.

The Islamic summit meeting began the following morning at the Hilton Hotel. There had been an unforeseen problem when the Pakistani delegation objected to India's participation. I was on a committee that was formed to mediate the quarrel, but our efforts were of no use: India was not allowed to participate. Thus, the whole of the first day of the conference was wasted in an attempt to solve the dispute between Pakistan and India.

The next morning, while still at my residence, I received a phone call from King Hussein. He said: "I shall come by, brother Anwar, in exactly five minutes, to accompany you on your visit to the Shah of Iran." I was astonished. "That is not what we agreed upon, brother Hussein," I replied. "I asked you very clearly to arrange my meeting with the shah to take place at your residence, not his. The meeting should take place on neutral ground. If I go to him, I shall be at a disadvantage. I don't want him to come to me, either. And even if I did, he would not accept."

King Hussein was silent for a moment. Then he replied: "What shall I do now? I have already arranged with the shah that we go to him. He is looking forward to your visit." I said to Hussein: "I honestly don't know how to get out of this awkward situation. I made it very clear to you right from the start that I wanted the meeting to take place with you." Hussein answered unhappily: "All right, Anwar, I'll try and find a solution." We hung up and eventually made our way to the Hilton for the next session of the conference. I found that King Hussein had broached the subject with the shah, asking him to change the place of our meeting. The shah had turned down the suggestion, and it was never brought up again. We had still not had our meeting, therefore, when the session began. When my turn came to speak for Egypt, I attacked no one. I said we had come to examine a problem of the utmost concern to Muslims everywhere. It was up to us to sit as brothers, in absolute harmony, having shed our differences outside the conference hall.

The shah's speech followed immediately afterward. He delivered it in French, his first foreign language (English being his second). I understand French very well, although I cannot speak it fluently, and I was very perturbed when the shah ended his speech with an inconsequential proposal, unworthy of being heard by those who had traveled such long distances to examine an issue of major importance. The Organization of African Unity (OAU) had already held its conference on the subject and had issued a strong condemnation of Israel's action. The shah's proposals, in contrast, were wholly unacceptable.

I could not remain silent. As soon as the shah had finished, I raised my hand, asking to speak. I made an angry, improvised response. "I have just listened to the resolutions proposed by the shah," I said. "All I can say is they are not worthy of the issue we are considering and are inferior to those made by the OAU. It is shameful that the shah, a Muslim emperor, should put forward such resolutions. The Islamic people will be ashamed when they hear them." And I ended by saying: "I do not forget the determination with which the shah's father struggled to maintain his independence during the Second World War, nor the resolution with which he opposed the designs of the Allies, who punished him for his stand by having him deposed."

I looked over at the shah, whose face was suffused with anger at what he had heard me say. During my speech, which was in Arabic, he had put on earphones to listen to an interpretation of my words in French. In that language, my words had carried an undertone of violence which I had not intended. When the time came for him to speak again, the shah strongly defended himself, emphasizing that he had struggled to confront imperialism and recover his country's land. Furthermore, he pointed out, his country depended neither on Great Britain nor on America. But Egypt, he said, leaned heavily on the Soviet Union.

I realized that the shah had misunderstood my words because of the French interpretation. Anxious to remedy this, I asked once more for permission to speak. King Hassan of Morocco assented, and I took the floor. "I am still of the opinion that the resolutions proposed by the shah are not sufficiently strong to deal with the grave incident that has brought us here," I said. "On the other hand, I suspect that due to a fault in the French translation, the shah did not fully grasp my meaning. I shall therefore remedy this by summarizing my feelings in a verse of Persian poetry."

The Arab heads of delegation were horror-struck. Behind me, Labib Shukair made a loud commotion with his feet, trying in alarm to warn me. They all thought I would make a fool of myself. Nobody knew that I not only spoke Persian but was also so familiar with Persian poetry that I could now, in one verse, summarize my response to the shah's speech. Paying no attention to the alarm around me, and ignoring Labib Shukair's hysterical behavior, I recited the verse. Translated into English, it says: "He who earns his bread by the sweat of his brow needs favors from no one."

The shah understood. Rising immediately to his feet, he began to applaud. Seeing this, the heads of state followed suit and applauded too. The Afghan prime minister, my friend Nour Ahmed el-E'timadi, who also spoke Persian, joined in. The shah's reaction was strange: he was at odds with Egypt, and my response to his speech and my objections to the resolutions he had proposed had angered him. Nevertheless, when I recited the verse in Persian, he had stood up and applauded. Labib Shukair could not believe his eyes. Later, he told me he had been on the verge of fainting when he heard me start to recite the Persian verse. He had not known I had once studied Persian and had imagined my pronunciation would be poor and my meaning distorted. But when he heard the shah applaud, he took a sheet of paper and wrote: "What you have done is most splendid."

Once the hall had quieted down, I asked permission to leave as I was obliged to return to Cairo. As I made my way toward the exit, I passed in front of the shah's seat. The shah was known never to have laughed and smiled only with difficulty. But now, thinking I was going over to him, he gave me a welcoming and encouraging smile. I contented myself with a quick wave of my hand and continued toward the exit.

I was accompanied to the airport by King el-Hassan's personal representative, Ahmed Balafrig, one of the best and most cultured of men, who said to me: "You cannot imagine how pleased I am, brother Anwar, at what you have done today. I never imagined you could exhibit such a command of Persian poetry as to move the shah to stand up and applaud. Many delegates praised your pronunciation." During a stopover in Tripoli on my way back, a reporter from the newspaper *al-Ahram* asked me, his face revealing doubt: "Is it true that you recited a poem in Persian and that the shah was so impressed that he stood up and applauded you at length?"

"Yes, that is indeed what happened," I replied. He did not appear to believe me, for he handed me a piece of paper and said: "If so, would you please write the verse in Persian on this sheet?" I did so with great ease.

But the Egyptian newspapers did not report a single word of the matter. The establishment which at that time controlled the press had ordered that it be ignored. Nevertheless, when I returned home I found that Nasser had heard about the incident from one of the Arab newspapers printed in Beirut, which he was in the habit of reading before he went to bed. I went to see Nasser primarily about his health and upon entering his bedroom found him surrounded by three physicians. As soon as he saw me, he asked me teasingly: "What's the story, Anwar?" I responded in surprise: "What story, Gamal?" He said jokingly, "The story of the Persian language and Persian poetry. I swear to you Anwar, I was in fits of laughter when I read it. I said to myself: 'Anwar recited any old nonsense, pretending it was Persian, and must have fooled them.' "

I laughed in turn, then said: "How could I get away with that, Gamal? I spoke in front of the Shah of Iran as well as other delegates whose official language is Persian." Gamal persisted: "I might have believed that if it had been just a few spoken sentences—but for you to recite Persian verse, well that is something I could never imagine from you, Anwar." We laughed for a long time and Nasser ordered that the story be published in the Egyptian papers.

After I took over following Nasser's death, Iran was among the first countries with which I wished to restore normal relations. I wrote a letter to the shah, the first part of which was in Arabic, the last in Persian. The shah promptly returned that gesture with another: in place of a typewritten reply, he sent one in his own handwriting. He welcomed my invitation to come to Egypt, and his visit with the shahbanu proved the start of a solid friendship that grew stronger by the day and firmer with each passing situation, and which lasted until the very last day of the shah's life.

During my stopover in Teheran in October 1971 I drew a quick picture for the shah of the situation facing Egypt at that time. We talked about the attitude of the United States and of the Soviet Union, whom we considered at that time as a friend. "Tell me about your position," I said to the shah. "The Americans sell arms to you. The Soviet Union stands on your frontier and also sells you arms. This can please neither friend nor foe."

The shah spoke at length about the situation and ended

with the words: "My advice to you, Anwar, is just to relax. Great powers will be great powers. They will never change." I replied: "That's true. I agree with you—but that doesn't mean I have to give in to whatever the great powers propose for me. My one and only aim at this stage is to prepare for the battle we are planning against Israel and which we intend to start very soon. No power in the world, great or small, will prevent us." And so I gave the shah advance warning of our intentions, which culminated in the October War of 1973. I bade him farewell and headed for Moscow.

On my return, we agreed to put an end to the disagreements between Egypt and Iran. Offices and embassies were reopened in Cairo and Teheran, and relations between two friendly countries were restored. The shah and shahbanu came to Egypt at my invitation, visiting Cairo and Upper Egypt. A strong and solid friendship sprang up between us. What the shah did for Egypt I can never forget or ignore—on the contrary, I let no occasion go by without mentioning his efforts on our behalf.

I recall particularly the crisis we faced when our oil supplies ran out at the end of the battle in October 1973. Qadaffi had betrayed us and sent our tankers back empty from Tobruk. We appealed to Saudi Arabia, but they had asked the minister of petroleum to fly out to discuss the request—all of which would take time we could ill afford. I therefore cabled the shah and said: "We are facing a crisis. Our oil will not last fifteen days. Please come to our rescue." The shah was up to the responsibility. Accurately assessing the drastic situation we were in, he immediately ordered tankers on the high seas to change course and head directly for Alexandria where they would discharge their loads of oil. Meanwhile, I received a cable from the shah in which he said: "On the way to you now are 600 tons of oil which were being shipped to Europe. I hope you will send the minister of petroleum to Iran so he can inform us what further oil you require."

Such was the treatment I received from the Arabs and such from the Shah of Iran. In an article attacking the Arabs, the late Lebanese reporter, Selim el-Lozy, wrote: "Egypt is fighting for you. Oil is the only thing your land possesses, yet you refuse to supply Egypt with any of it, obliging her to turn instead to the Iranians." As it turned out, Saudi Arabia did eventually send us some oil—for which we were grateful. But had the shah not stood by us we would have been faced with a problem which God only knows how we would have borne.

At my invitation, the shah later came to Egypt. It was only natural that our talks should center around the war that had just been fought and the programs I was considering next. The shah was very enthusiastic about the construction and development program I had in mind. To my surprise, he said: "I would like, on behalf of my country, to participate in the rebuilding and revival of the city of Port Said. I hope you will accept a loan of two hundred and fifty million dollars, to be repaid over a long term, to be used for the construction of Port Said as a free zone to promote world trade." It was another surprise from the shah and one that truly embarrassed me. Not only had he rescued us from our predicament by sending us oil, but here he was again voluntarily offering aid for the revival of Port Said, which had sustained the horrors of all the previous wars. I thanked the shah and our friendship grew stronger and firmer.

Ours was not just a personal friendship but extended beyond that to the official level. Egypt and Iran were the two oldest countries and the most ancient civilizations in the region. The Iranian Empire was created twenty-five hundred years ago, at a time when Europe was still divided into provinces that had not yet attained the status of independent countries. Egypt was a country with a government of its own as far back as seven thousand years ago. Because of this bond between our two countries, the shah and I agreed to coordinate our affairs to establish a balance of power in the region, whereby no foreign power would be allowed to interfere with or alter its borders. For we were the "owners" and therefore best aware of the interests of its peoples.

The shah based his stand on the great military power Iran possessed at that time. Egypt also had the basic ingredients of such power and was working hard to realize its potential. The shah and I agreed that decisions would be taken, not by the great powers, but by the countries of the region themselves. At that time, I was trying to find a solution to the problem of the three islands in the Persian Gulf over which the Arabs and Iranians were in dispute. I told the shah: "An alliance between Egypt and Iran is not enough. It is only right that the Arabs and the Persians also unite, for they are natural allies, brought together by geography, religion, and destiny. We should strive to create such an alliance so that we can maintain our independence and confront any challenge, be it from the East or from the West. Our region boasts over sixty percent of the oil reserves in the world—enormous wealth, which must be safeguarded. This cannot be realized unless we unite." The shah agreed, and I went on to say: "For this reason, we must work to settle our own differences. We should begin with the problem of the islands, to which a solution must be found."

An opportunity to do this came toward the end of my visit to Teheran when Sheikh Zayed of the United Arab Emirates requested that we meet. Iran had seized control of three Arab islands in the Persian Gulf: Great Tomb, Smaller Tomb, and Abou Moussa. These three islands are the property of one of the states that forms the UAE. On the spot, after being informed of Sheikh Zayed's request to meet me, I decided to bring up this topic in my discussions with the shah. I managed to convince him the problem had to be solved, although the shah was quite sensitive about it. My line of reasoning centered on the argument that the bond of Islam which united us impelled us to settle all our outstanding problems. When I felt the shah had grown convinced of this, I went to see Sheikh Zayed at his residence in Teheran. He had at first insisted on calling at my guest house, but I told his people I would come to him instead.

I went there on my way to the airport before my departure for Saudi Arabia and told Sheikh Zayed of all that had taken place during my meeting with the shah. I informed him: "I have managed to find a solution to the problem with Mohamed [the shah] before you asked it of me." I have never before commented on my success at that time in mediating between Iran and the Emirates over the problem of the islands because I didn't want it to become a forum for political auctioneering.

A few months afterward, I traveled as usual to Aswan to survey the construction projects in the south. I made sure I carried out this visit annually to see on the spot how the projects were progressing in that part of the country away from Cairo. It was not for leisure or a holiday at a resort. Nor did I stay in a palatial mansion, but in a guest house for engineers of Aswan. While I was still there, at the beginning of January 1978, a sudden dispatch came from the Shah of Iran. It said: "I am coming to spend one night in Aswan, then I will return home." Though I welcomed the shah, I was surprised at this impromptu visit because I had been with him in Iran only a few months before, and he had visited me in Cairo, so what was the urgency of such a visit? At the Aswan airport, I greeted the shah warmly, and the shah reciprocated by saying: "I came for one simple reason: to announce to the world my support for your peace initiative. For this reason, I will not spend more than twenty-four hours here, after which I shall return home." I felt a deep gratitude to the man for making that effort to affirm his stand, and I told him: "Why should you take this burden upon yourself? You have already announced your position, and you have always stood by Egypt in its previous crises, both during and after the October War. We will never forget your supplying us with oil when we needed it then."

I recall this now to refute what a well-known journalist, a friend of world leaders, claimed in a recent television interview that was telecast in London. He said that the Shah of Iran had never done anything to help Egypt. But he forgot the shah's stand that I have just mentioned. He also forgot that the shah had supplied us with buses when we were in desperate need of them to solve our country's transportation problems. The story of that deal started when I asked the shah: "Is it true, Mohamed, that you can produce Mercedes buses in Iran?" He replied: "Yes." Then I asked: "Can you send us three hundred buses?" And he replied: "Yes, send me your team of experts and the buses you ask for will be in Egypt as soon as possible."

On yet another occasion, the then prime minister of Egypt, Abdel Aziz Hegazy, informed me that the cotton crop would not be sold that year and that we would therefore run short of hard currency. Immediately, I told him to be in touch with the Shah of Iran and ask for a loan with the cotton as guarantee. Hegazy carried out my instructions and sent a Telex to Iran asking for the loan. The shah replied personally: "How much do you need exactly?" We informed him we needed 50 million dollars. The shah said: "The money is on its way. As for the cotton crop, keep it in your stores so that you can sell it later."

All of these past actions were present in my mind while I

was with the shah that year in Aswan. He told me there: "The reason behind my visit is not only to announce before the world my support for your initiative but to convey this support specifically to the Arab world. My intention is to go to Jeddah and to meet with King Khalid and the Saudi princes and to tell them openly: 'What are you waiting for? Why don't you announce your support for Sadat's initiative? Sadat is not only working for Egypt but for the entire Arab world and for you." And the Shah of Iran actually did fly to Jeddah and told them: "Why don't you announce openly your support of the peace process? Sadat is working for the whole area, for a comprehensive and just peace, and for the return of Arab rights."

A whole year passed. And again I received the shah in Aswan, in January 1979, in the same city, at the same airport, with the same hotel as his residence.

But the shah was not the shah I knew, and Iran had become another Iran.

In January 1978, the shah had made his flying visit to Aswan to announce his wholehearted support for my peace initiative and to tell all Arabs to support it. But in January 1979 the shah had come to Egypt to seek refuge. In the span of a single year, his situation had been transformed.

When he had returned to Teheran in January 1978 after his short visit to Aswan, a plot was awaiting him, hatched by the Iranian Left. I say that because anyone who has a little knowledge of politics would arrive at the conclusion that the Left was behind all the moves against the shah. The Iranian Left had decided to wage its battle against the shah on the streets of Teheran—one of its well-known tactics. It starts by organizing a demonstration, when clashes take place between police and demonstrators. The clash develops into an exchange of shots with a number of victims among the demonstrators.

With the greatest precision, the Left goes on with its tactics. During the funeral procession of the victims, other clashes take place, and more victims fall. And on the fortieth day of mourning for the victims, more demonstrations take place and more victims die. And this vicious circle never ends . . . demonstrations followed by clashes and victims, and so on. But for the Left—which had instigated all this—the important thing was that the explosive situation should continue between the shah and the Iranian public. The aim of their tactics was to exert pressure on the shah and to blackmail him. And when the shah started to submit, his political opponents simply intensified their pressure in order to secure further gains.

I hope I am not misunderstood. I don't mean to support the shah against a popular revolution, since this is an internal issue of concern only to the people of Iran and I don't want to interfere with it. And I am certainly not against the revolution of any people since I myself made my revolution—and indeed was ready to repeat it on September 5 of this year if the situation called for it.* All I want to say, without interfering in the internal affairs of Iran, is that the Left was behind the popular revolt in the streets of Teheran, pushing matters to an extreme from February 1978 to January 1979. And the result was the shah taking refuge in Egypt.

When he arrived in Aswan with his wife, Empress Farah, he was very ill, and I left the emperor and empress to rest at their hotel. Next day, Jihan (Mrs. Sadat) and I went to

---

*Editor's note: This is a reference to the unrest in Egypt that preceded Sadat's assassination and which was followed by the arrest and detention of several leading dissidents.

pay them a visit. We found the empress still asleep, and she stayed asleep until the early afternoon. The shah apologized to us and said: "We have not slept soundly for a whole year."

The shah, as I said, had lived under tremendous pressures and faced all kinds of demonstrations instigated by the Left: sometimes student demonstrations, sometimes women's demonstrations, and sometimes children's demonstrations. And of course he could not attack children. The shah's mistake was to retreat and start submitting to the demands of the Left. For example, they forced him to abolish the Iranian calendar year, Niroz, and to adopt the Muslim calendar year. But the shah's basic mistake was made when he abolished the multiparty system and formed one party in its place. This decision meant he was resisting the course of history, and the course of history can never be stopped, because if you try, history defies you.

In the nineteenth and early twentieth centuries, it may have been possible to resort to the one-party system, as during Ataturk's and Hitler's and Mussolini's time, but to resort to it these days is a fatal mistake. The course of history allows only for a transition from a one-party to a multiparty system, and it does not allow for the opposite, because one is a step forward and the other a step backward. When the shah committed this mistake, all forces at once joined ranks against him, leading to an alliance of all his opponents. They were thus all grouped in one camp: Bazergan and Bani Sadr, the Left and "Mogahedi Khalq." All joined ranks to topple the shah.

When the shah arrived in Aswan, I felt he would never return to Iran, as events subsequently confirmed. I met him at the foot of the steps of his aircraft and told him: "Rest assured, Mohamed, you are in your country and with your people and brothers." But he was in a state of shock and his eyes were brimful of tears. En route to the hotel, while still shedding tears, he told me about the farewell of his soldiers at the Teheran airport and how one soldier took hold of him and said, "Don't leave us. Iran will be lost without you and the future is dark."

I immediately asked the shah: "Why don't you withdraw the aircraft of your air force and your naval units from Iran?" My reason for making this suggestion was that the army, the fleet, and the air force had remained loyal to the shah and stayed loyal until the arrival of Khomeini. I was prepared to offer them sanctuary in Egypt. I told the shah: "Egypt is prepared to be their host until conditions stabilize in Iran." His reply was the reply of a man who had lost all hope and any ability to take a decision. He told me: "America will not agree. They will not allow me to do it. I am not able to take such a decision."

I then knew that the rule of the shah had ended and that his return to Iran had become impossible.

The shah told me, while he was still weeping, that he felt like a leader who had deserted the battlefield. But he was forced to leave Iran because the Americans had exerted a great deal of pressure on him. He told me how the American ambassador came to meet him and kept looking at his watch and telling him that "every minute that passes and delays your departure is not in your interest and not in the interest of Iran . . . you have to hasten your departure, immediately."

The reason behind this American stand was that Carter's policy was based on a belief in human rights, and he considered that the shah's presence in Iran was against the will of the Iranian people and against Iranian human rights. During their summit conference that year, the four Western leaders—Carter, Schmidt, D'Estaing, and Callaghan—all took a stand against the shah. This stand led to the departure of the shah from Iran and the return of Khomeini. The Western leaders did not realize that they were installing a time bomb inside Iran. They did not grasp what they had done until after it had exploded, with its shrapnel raining all over Iran.

· 3 ·

MY VIEWS OF KHOMEINI

What has happened in Iran, and what is happening there today, is no surprise to me. Several years have passed since the revolution, but matters still go from bad to worse. I cannot foretell the future, but I can interpret what I see. And I do not exclude some sudden and startling development. I do not exclude the possibility of the extreme Left grabbing power from Khomeini. I do not exclude the possibility of the Iranian armed forces making a move to end the rule of the Ayatollah. When everything has been lost, when darkness prevails and terror rules, then anything becomes possible.

When the revolution occurred, Khomeini claimed it was an Islamic revolution. I thought: "No, this is not an Islamic revolution. It is a Khomeinian revolution, built upon revenge, blood, and terror."

Khomeini was given a great opportunity to realize the dreams of his people. He could have built a great country. Iran could have become a miraculously strong power, respected by the whole world. Unfortunately, the chance was missed and Khomeini has taken his country down with him into the abyss. When he took over the country, Iran exported 6.5 million barrels of oil a day—worth about $200 million or $73 billion in a full year. Did Khomeini need more treasure than this with which to build up his country?

The main objective of a revolution should be to look after the welfare of the people. But this did not happen after the revolution in Iran, for many reasons. Khomeini wished to build up popular support; so he called his revolution an Islamic revolution. This was a lie, as was proved when he turned to bloody revenge to settle his personal disputes. Khomeini's style is not the style of Islam. It is also a fact that those who threw out the shah and brought Khomeini into power are Communists of the extreme Left. Khomeini welcomed their support at first; at that time he would have welcomed support from the devil himself.

When I saw he was being used by the extreme Left, and when I saw the methods he was using to rule the country, I forecast that one day Khomeini would be forced to drink from the same cup from which he forced the shah to drink. It is naïve to believe the situation in Iran is directed solely by Khomeini. The truth is that the country is in the hands of those who brought him home from exile—those who blew up his party headquarters, killing dozens of his closest associates. Matters will go from bad to worse. Sooner or later those who are bringing about the chaos in Iran will overthrow Khomeini and take over the country. When Khomeini returned to Iran he was received with adulation by millions of people. But behind it all was the hand of the extreme Left. They had laid their plans at least a year before they brought him home.

The Communists began their campaign by fomenting discontent against the shah. They organized most of the demonstrations and the attacks on property. The shah's security forces were compelled to intervene, and this was then used as an excuse for the next day's rioting. The Communists thereby destabilized the situation and took the initiative away from the shah. They went so far as to organize a huge demonstration of very young children, who were marched to the shah's palace in the hope that the shah would shoot them. The Communists calculated this would cause even more outrage against the shah and create chaos. That is what they wanted. The mistake Khomeini made was to rely on this same group of people who had created the volatile situation for the shah. He should have set them aside, but he did not. He forgot that those who brought him to power could just as easily throw him out.

The Communists are very strong. The proof of it came when Khomeini did finally try to escape from their grasp, and when they responded by giving him a terrible warning. They blew up his party headquarters and left the bodies of his most important supporters and allies inside. This was done solely to demonstrate to Khomeini that they were in control and to show the outside world that Khomeini does not in fact rule Iran. That this has happened is Khomeini's own fault. He failed to control the situation from the first. Had he done so, the crisis over the American embassy hostages would not have happened.

There was in fact a very close relationship between the embassy hostages crisis and the struggle for power in Iran. Those who created the hostage crisis were a group of leftist students. For one whole year Khomeini was powerless to intervene. The leftists laughed at him. The Communists were clever enough to inflate Khomeini's importance by pretending their orders came directly from him. By using this pretext they were able to prevent government ministers and even the president from intervening. Khomeini himself knew they were mocking him and that they would not adhere to any real orders he issued. The true masters of the situation were the Communist leadership. Anyone who understands the basis of politics will realize that neither Khomeini nor the president nor the prime minister rules Iran today. Those who rule that country are the people who control the mob.

I therefore challenge the claim that Iran has become an Islamic republic. I have studied Islam's role in politics and government and I recently read a book on the subject by Dr. Mahmoud Metawli. In it he demonstrates that there is in fact no Islamic political system. Our rules for life are based on the holy Koran; what we take from it is implemented without political discussion. A second element in the life of a Muslim is our interpretation of the practices of the Prophet Muhammad. This commits us to two things in politics: the ruler must consult with his people about his government, but decisions about government must remain with the ruler. There is nothing in the Koran that calls for presidential or parliamentary rule. So where does Khomeini get his idea that his is an Islamic system? There is nothing constitutional about what he has done. In any country in the world, there cannot be anyone higher in the political sense than the president or head of state—except the people.

During the pilgrimage season, the people of Iran have been taught to shout religious slogans that equate Khomeini with God. "God is great!" they cry, "Khomeini is great!" How can we accept as head of state a sheikh who wears a turban and makes a god of himself, who claims he is not liable to mistakes, and whose decisions are above question? Today, under many royal systems of government, the king reigns but does not rule. Under a presidential system, the constitution provides for the president to be questioned. In Egypt, for example, I as President can be impeached. All these systems of government recognize that rulers are human. But Khomeini puts himself above all that. Is it possible to call this the rule of Islam?

Iran has fallen into complete chaos. Look, for example, at

what happened to the Republic's first president, Bani Sadr. He was brought to office by Khomeini, then removed by him. In the first instance, 80 percent of the population of Teheran were brought out to demonstrate in his favor. In the second instance the same 80 percent turned out to demand his head. It is best that governments are not run by religious leaders. This is not to say a religious man should not rule, provided he has the necessary experience. What I reject is a ruler who comes to power solely because he is a sheikh with a turban. What is so horrible about Khomeini is that he fights with the sword of bitterness and ruthless revenge. The practices of Islam do not teach us to bring about a blood bath.

Khomeini could have ruled over a society as wealthy as any in the world. But he built up a system that was ignorant and corrupt. He went to war with Iraq, which destroyed his oil refineries. He has taken away his people's sense of values. He inherited large industries, but where are they today?

All this contributes to internal discontent. I hope that those who still believe Khomeini has brought about an Islamic revolution can now see this. If for only one hour there were the rule of reason in Iran, someone would stand up and say: "Look, people, we are one of the richest countries of the world. How could this have happened to us? How can we have four and one-half million people unemployed while during the shah's time we had to import labor from abroad? Why do we have to import petroleum products from abroad, when once we exported six and one-half million barrels of oil each day?"

Unfortunately, Khomeini has removed the rule of reason. I remember the same thing happening when I came to office in 1970; my own people were living on their emotions. I immediately called for the rule of reason and was faced with fierce resistance from those who had ruled Egypt through slogans. But I learned that the Left loses all its weapons when the rule of reason prevails. This is why they reject logic and organize emotional demonstrations based on slogans.

Do I think what has happened in Iran could be repeated in other Islamic countries? No, I do not. Personally, I think it is impossible. We live in an interrelated world, linked by speedy communications. Anyone who has followed Khomeini's revolution feels sorry for what will happen to the people of Iran. They do not wish to see it repeated in their own country. From the first, Khomeini uttered a huge lie, which he may have believed himself. He thought he had achieved a miracle when he took over the country from the shah. When millions came out to greet him, he believed himself a god. So he announced that his mission was not confined to Iran but would also be exported abroad. He involved the Iranian people in this mirage. But he neglected his country. So is it possible that any other nation could admire the experience of the Iranian people under Khomeini? Or think to copy it?

I sometimes wonder how it came about that the leaders of other Islamic countries remained silent through the chaos that was happening under the banner of religion in Iran. I am reminded of what happened last year in Mecca when terrorists seized the Prophet's tomb. The United States was the first to announce the news that this had happened. The Saudi authorities said nothing. Immediately, Khomeini seized the opportunity to say the United States was behind the deed. This was a serious accusation, but no one reproached him for it. In the end, I was compelled to do so myself, in spite of the silence of my Arab brothers. I also reproached my Saudi brothers because they did not reveal the whole truth of what had happened and failed to make it clear that the United States was not involved in the conspiracy in any way. The result was that some people believed Khomeini's accusations. Demonstrations erupted against the American embassy in Pakistan and in other Arab and Islamic countries.

I want every Islamic country to announce its rejection of Khomeini's abuses, his terrorism, his vengefulness, and the destruction that he seeks to export. I think the League of Islamic and Arab States could play an important part in this. I am not asking them to interfere in Iran's internal affairs but to recognize that we Muslims should abide by the teachings of our religion. When Khomeini stands up and says his oppression and terror are an Islamic revolution, we should oppose him and tell him that he does not represent Islam.

·4·

CONFLICT WITH COLONEL QADAFFI

I was greatly impressed by Colonel Qadaffi the first time I met him, finding him full of enthusiasm, nationalism, and idealism. I told Nasser that those who had carried out the Libyan revolution would lead their country and its people to peace. How deceived I was in the person of Muammar al-Qadaffi! I discovered he had a double personality: the first impressing you with its idealism, enthusiasm and devotion; the second appalling you with its evil, bitterness, violence, and bloodthirstiness. He is the embodiment of the personality known as Dr. Jekyll and Mr. Hyde.

I first met him during a stopover in Tripoli on the way back from the Rabat summit in September 1969, the same month that the Libyan revolution had taken place. I arrived in Tripoli at night. Muammar al-Qadaffi received me as soon as I stepped from the plane. I was genuinely pleased at the meeting, which gave me a complete picture of the Libyan revolution and those who had planned and executed it.

Qadaffi revealed to me the secrets of the Libyan underground movement, confiding that they had attempted to reproduce the Egyptian Free Officers' movement which had led our revolution in 1952. They had even taken on the personalities of the Free Officers, distributing their roles among themselves. Muammar had assumed the role of Gamal Abdel Nasser, Mustafa el-Kharubi that of Abdel Hakim Amer, and so on. I learned from Qadaffi that they had read every word that had been written on the July 23 revolution in Egypt and on those who had taken part in it. Qadaffi reminded me of my story in the newspaper *al-Goumhouria* on the July revolution and its secrets. As he spoke, I noticed he remembered every word I had written.

I was genuinely impressed by the men of the Libyan revolution. Accompanying Qadaffi was his associate, Abdul Salam Jallud, who was wearing simple overalls. I did not discover until later that he had been Qadaffi's second-in-command in the revolution. After dining with Qadaffi, I took my leave of him in order to board my plane and resume my trip back to Cairo. To my surprise, they all insisted that I make a second stopover, this time at the Benghazi airport, to meet their associate, Mustafa el-Kharubi, who had assumed the role Abdel Hakim Amer had played in the Free Officers' movement. Qadaffi asked me to take along a number of Libyan ministers who were on their way to Benghazi.

As it was nighttime, the plane would not arrive in Benghazi before 1:00 A.M., and I imagined there would be no more than a short stopover. The ministers who had boarded my plane at Tripoli would disembark and I would then continue my flight to Cairo. Imagine my surprise, therefore, when after the plane had landed at Benghazi, a youth boarded it and, approaching me, threw himself into my arms and embraced me. He introduced himself, saying: "I am Mustafa el-Kharubi." I laughed and said: "Hello, Abdel Hakim Amer!" He said, insistently: "You must come down with me." I objected, saying: "No, Mustafa, my son, it is late. I have an hour ahead of me before I reach Cairo. It has been a long and exhausting day."

Mustafa el-Kharubi brushed aside my objections, urging and insisting that I go down with him. In the end, I had to comply. Mustafa el-Kharubi introduced me to the officers who stood in line, saying: "I present to you Anwar el-Sadat, one of the heroes of the July revolution." I very quickly forgot my weariness in my genuine pleasure at meeting el-Kharubi and his men. I did not glance at the hands of my watch as they advanced to announce the break of dawn. I returned to Cairo feeling elated and greatly impressed by Qadaffi and his group. They had brought back memories of youth with what they had done and intended to do.

In Cairo, I went to see Nasser to tell him about the Libyans and their revolution, saying: "I was truly impressed by those youngsters. I was even more impressed by their nationalism and enthusiasm, as well as their devotion to the people of their country. I believe, Gamal, our part has been played. I advise you to send for two or three of those boys so that you can work with them. They belong to the future: as for us, we are finished. We have fought our battles and the time has now come for us to step down." We laughed. Gamal Abdel Nasser said: "You admire those boys to that extent, Anwar?" I replied, emphatically: "To that extent, Gamal. Soon you will meet them yourself. Then I will hear what you have to say about them."

The days passed. At Nasser's invitation, Muammar al-Qadaffi came to visit us in Cairo. In the salon at Nasser's house I turned to Gamal, saying: "I hope, Mr. President, that you will repeat to Muammar what I previously told you about him and his brothers." Addressing Muammar, Gamal said: "Anwar is a great admirer of yours. He has advised me to send for two or three of you so that we can both retire."

That was my initial opinion of Qadaffi. As I said, I was greatly impressed by him. I expected much from him and his brothers in the service of their country and the Arab nation at large. This remained my opinion until I suddenly discovered Qadaffi had a double personality. As much as there was sweetness and kindness in the first personality, there was viciousness and hatred in the second. I can never forget what he did to us before and after the October War. We were dealing with his second personality, discovering faults rarely found in a normal person.

Following the cease-fire in October 1973, Hilal, the Egyptian minister of petroleum, came to me and said: "Our entire oil reserves throughout the country will last only fifteen days at most." The news was a national disaster. We had not yet reached an agreement on disengagement; there was every likelihood that the situation would flare up and the battle be resumed. I expected little good from our so-called "ally and brother" Muammar Qadaffi, for my experiences with him were leading me to distrust his every promise. He had undertaken to send us spare parts for our Mirage planes, but none had turned up. Time and time again, he had given his word but never kept it.

I knew that the Dassault factory, which manufactures Mirage planes in France, did not provide spare parts upon request. One had to wait at least six months to receive them. That was in August, two months before the war—and the peak of the European holiday season, when factories come to a standstill, shops close, and offices are emptied of their employees. I sent a representative to France to open negotiations. I told them we were ready to spend a million pounds over and above the cost price of the spare parts. For what is a million pounds in the context of a destiny such as ours? The representative left for Paris, and the negotiations began.

Later, on October 4, 1973, it so happened that Qadaffi's confidant, Abdul Salam Jallud, paid a visit to Cairo. I summoned him and said: "Abdul Salam, cut short your holiday in Egypt, return to your country, and say this to Muammar: The hour of battle is drawing very near, I shall not specify the exact date, but it is enough for him to know that the battle is imminent. All I am asking from Libya is: First: In the event that Israel should bomb the port of Alexandria, the Libyan port of Tobruk should become a substitute, so that supplies can be landed there and transported to Egypt overland. Second: We need four million tons of oil from Libya over a period of a year and a half. Third: We need spare parts for Mirage planes."

We had already taken steps to prepare the way for the first of my requests. Trucks had traveled to Tobruk and then returned to Alexandria, allowing us to calculate the distance and the time needed to get supplies through. The reason for the second request was that as we prepared for battle it was vital that we shut down our Morgan oil fields in the Gulf of Suez, as they were vulnerable to Israeli artillery. This meant that we would be unable to cover our oil requirements.

And this brings to mind a story. I knew that closing down the Morgan fields and extinguishing the flares would confirm our intentions to the Israelis. So as not to alert them, I instructed Hilal, the minister of petroleum, to put out the flares only half an hour before the battle began. Hilal reported back: "In order to carry out your instructions, we must consider two alternatives in the event that the Israelis bomb the field. The first is that we are prepared to sacrifice the lives of the field workers; the second is that in order to save their lives, we evacuate them from the danger zone before the start of the battle."

I said to Hilal: "Do not sacrifice the life of a single worker, whether Egyptian or foreign. Put into effect your plan to safeguard them all. But make sure you close down the field and extinguish the flares half an hour before zero hour." To this day, nobody knows the story of how engineer Hilal, on his own initiative, flew a plane over the oil field just before the battle, as though he were on a normal tour of inspection. His plan was 100 percent successful; no workers were exposed to danger of any sort.

Which brings me back to our request to Qadaffi. I had imagined he would agree to provide us with oil for a year to come because I was preparing myself and my country for a long war. In fact, I insisted on prolonging it, because I knew full well Israel could not stand a drawn-out conflict. Qadaffi had just nationalized the British Petroleum Company—the only company with oil fields close to the Egyptian border, producing 10 million tons of oil a year, which was pumped to Tobruk for shipment abroad in tankers. I asked Qadaffi to set aside 4 million tons of that oil, to be sent to us via Tobruk.

I had already taken precautions to obtain spare parts for the twenty-five Mirage planes, but those planes used up spare parts like fire. Without a large reserve of spare parts, planes would be of no use in a battle. So I repeated my request to Abdul Salam Jallud, who cut short his holiday and returned to Tripoli, bearing my message to Qadaffi. From Tripoli came the message: "Rest assured, we have approved your three requests."

The war began two days later. The first day went by, then the second. We received a telephone call from Qadaffi, asking us to open up the Voice of the Arabs radio so that he could make a speech in support of Egypt and its armed forces. I agreed to this, and Qadaffi made an infamous speech, hurling insults upon us and predicting our defeat and Israel's victory. Eager to see us defeated, Qadaffi went out of his way to brake our wheels. He never did carry out his promises. We sent tankers that he had promised would be returned to us filled with oil. After only three shipments, he changed his mind. Much to our surprise, the tankers returned as empty as they had left. As luck would have it, the port at Alexandria was not hit; otherwise Qadaffi would certainly have refused to allow us to use Tobruk as a substitute. He never did send us the spare parts for the Mirage planes, as he had promised. On each occasion he had given his word but never kept it. These experiences have led me to mistrust everything he says.

While relations were still good between Egypt and Libya, Colonel Qadaffi asked me to supply him with two submarines to protect his country against danger. I complied with his request and sent two submarines from our navy. The submarines had Egyptian crews but took their orders directly from Colonel Qadaffi. One of these submarine commanders was soon to receive a very peculiar order. Qadaffi instructed him to go on a mission on the high seas and to wait there for a huge passenger liner. When it arrived, he was ordered to sink it. The commander obeyed the first part of his orders and sailed off into the high seas. According to accepted naval practice, he reported back by radio every two hours to Egyptian naval headquarters in Alexandria.

Once on the high seas the commander of the submarine reported back to Alexandria with the remainder of his order from Colonel Qadaffi. He told them he had been commanded to sink the British liner *Queen Elizabeth II* as she sailed through the Mediterranean Sea with a full complement of British and American passengers on their way to Israel to celebrate the twenty-fifth anniversary of the creation of the Jewish state.

At Alexandria, our naval command was astounded to hear of this frightful order Qadaffi had given. As usual when he gives these sorts of orders, Qadaffi leaves his office and retreats to his tent in the Libyan desert where no one can reach him. And there he stays until he is told his orders have been carried out. It was 1:30 P.M. on that day in 1973 when our naval command in Alexandria was in touch with me and told me of the orders that had been given to the submarine commander. They said he was on his way to the rendezvous to sink the liner in waters which were, incidentally, guarded by the American Sixth Fleet.

I asked them: "Can you contact the commander of the submarine?" They replied: "No, there is a radio blackout. We shall have to wait until he makes his next routine contact with us in two hours' time." I asked them: "Will the submarine have reached its objective by then?" They said: "No, not by then. We expect it will still be quite some distance away." I said: "Thank God! As soon as he is in touch with you give him orders from me personally that he is to abort his mission and head directly to our base in Alexandria." I asked them to inform me as soon as the submarine commander had received my orders. After two long hours the news came through: I received confirmation that my orders had been received and acknowledged and were being acted upon. The submarine was on its way back to Alexandria.

To explain this mania, we perhaps need to go back thirty years to a statement made by Sir Anthony Eden, then British prime minister. I remember his words today as clearly as when I first read them. "Arabs are exactly like children," he said. "When one of them screams you need to give him a tank or a gun to play with to stop the screaming." Today, this game has become too dangerous. Try to imagine what would have happened if Qadaffi had succeeded in sinking the *QE2*. First of all, Egypt would have lost its submarine and her crew. The Sixth Fleet would not have allowed it to escape. Secondly, the world would never have forgiven the Arabs for committing this criminal and barbaric act, involving innocent women and children who had nothing in the world to do with the Arab-

Israeli conflict. This would have been the shameful consequence of giving arms to a teen-ager—or a mad man. Qadaffi has the mentality of a small child. The tragedy is that the toys he plays with are real weapons.

This sort of action also makes me wonder about the incident in August 1981 when two Libyan planes were shot down by planes from the American Sixth Fleet. I would like to make one last remark about this incident to the Arab leaders who sent Qadaffi telegrams of support after his planes had been shot down: Do you not think of the seriousness of what this maniac is doing? Do you not think of the innocent lives that could be lost because of Qadaffi's dangerous games? Or have the lives of innocent people also become a game in the hands of our countries' rulers?

·5·

THE RANCOR OF NIKITA KHRUSHCHEV

During the summer of 1964 I was in President Nasser's home with Nasser and President Tito of Yugoslavia, along with a number of aides. We were all glued to a transistor radio following an exciting development in Moscow. Nasser listened carefully, concentrating deeply; Tito, in his dramatically nervous manner, was holding a cigarette lighter in his hand and kept rolling it and turning it upside down while listening. I imagine high-ranking officials around the entire world were following the same dramatic news: Nikita Khrushchev's portrait had been removed from the walls of Moscow, while the pictures of the rest of the Politburo remained. The Central Committee of the Soviet Communist Party had been unexpectedly convened in the middle of the summer vacation. Khrushchev, first secretary of the committee, was on holiday on the Black Sea and had not been invited to attend the meeting.

Of those present in Nasser's salon, I was the most happy at the news we were hearing. I knew the arrangements for Khrushchev's downfall were the work of a good friend of mine, Aleksei Shelepin, chairman of the Internal Security Committee. For his part, Nasser was worried by the fact that Khrushchev had finished a visit to Egypt only a few days earlier, and while he was here he had completed an agreement with Nasser permitting Egypt to buy advanced armaments from the Soviet Union and obliging Russia to contribute to the building up of the Egyptian economy. As for Tito, he seemed to be the most concerned of all, fearing a change in the Soviet leadership would undo Khrushchev's work in bringing about a reconciliation with Yugoslavia. Tito kept changing radio stations nervously, then switching back to the station he had been listening to in the first place.

At length, the news came through that Khrushchev had been removed from all his posts and that a collective leadership would take over, with Brezhnev as first secretary-general, Kosygin as premier, and Malenkov as head of the Presidium. I was delighted—first because my friend Shelepin had been the star in bringing all this about, and second because of my own relationship with Khrushchev. I had perceived the dominant element in his makeup to be one of rancor; he disliked me; and when he visited Egypt I had done all I could to avoid him. He was prone to harsh and foul language and was full of curses for all regimes that did not embrace communism.

Following the removal of Khrushchev from all his posts, however, Nasser made the decision to stand by him. Our press kept up a campaign of indirect attacks on the new regime, until at length the new collective became worried enough to send my old friend Shelepin to see us in Cairo. As chairman of the Internal Committee of the Soviet Communist party, Shelepin was in control of the country's internal security. When he arrived in Egypt, he looked relatively young and was envied by most of the other Soviet leaders, who were all older than he. I cherished my friendship with Shelepin and still believe the bilateral ties between Egypt and the Soviet

Union would never have deteriorated to the extent they did had the other leaders been more like him.

His visit to Cairo was a great success, and after his departure our press dropped their attacks, while Nasser promised to make a visit to Moscow later on. During his visit to Cairo, Shelepin had many meetings with Nasser and came one night to an informal dinner at the home of Field Marshal Abdel Hakim Amer, then commander of the Egyptian armed forces. "Tell us about what you have done to Khrushchev, and why," we said to Shelepin. But he in turn surprised us all by asking us a question instead: "You tell me first—was or was not Khrushchev rude to Iraqi President Abdul Rahman Aref when they were together in Aswan recently?"

Actually, Khrushchev had attacked Aref on a number of occasions at Aswan and had insulted the Iraqi leader in the most obscene words imaginable. But only a very few people had been present when these heated arguments took place; so we were taken by surprise at Shelepin's question. It transpired, however, that the news had somehow got back to Moscow, and the quarrel between Khrushchev and President Aref was among the main justifications used by the Soviet leadership for Khrushchev's overthrow.

The truth is they had really been taken aback by the overwhelming reception given to Khrushchev by the Egyptian people. He had been given a hero's welcome, on a scale that even Khrushchev himself could hardly have dreamed possible. Alarmed at this, the Moscow leadership thereupon decided on a swift removal before Khrushchev could capitalize on his image as a world hero. The two excuses they used were his outrageous behavior at Aswan and the failure of his agricultural policies at home.

The fact is of course that neither Khrushchev nor Brezhnev,

nor any other Communist leader, could solve the agricultural problem without making radical changes in his Marxist philosophy. This philosophy ignores one simple but crucial fact: that agriculture should never be nationalized, nor the farmers either. Before communism came to the Soviet Union, the Ukraine was known for its tremendous production of wheat, but after the land was nationalized the Soviet Union has had to import some 25 million tons of wheat every year just to keep her own people from famine.

But back to Khrushchev's visit to Egypt, where he had come to celebrate a historic occasion: the altering of the course of the Nile following the completion of the first stage of the Aswan High Dam.

Nasser had invited a number of world leaders to the celebrations, among them Khrushchev and President Aref of Iraq. Khrushchev delivered a speech at the Aswan stadium and distributed a number of medals—amazingly enough giving one to the chauffeur of the dam's engineer, Osman Ahmed Osman, without giving one to Osman himself. In his view, Osman was a member of the bourgeoisie and therefore did not deserve a medal, even though he was chairman of the nationalized board that had constructed the dam. After this ceremony, Khrushchev delivered his first attack on President Aref. I think his motivation was the legendary reception he had been given on his own arrival at Alexandria, which he used as an excuse to frighten his rivals in the Central Committee in Moscow.

Nasser and Field Marshal Amer rushed in to calm down Khrushchev after his outburst, and the first part of the celebration passed without disaster. Next, we flew to Bernice on the Red Sea, where the yacht *Syria* was anchored, and decided to spend the day in fishing and other recreational activities. During a political meeting on board the yacht, we were stunned to hear Khrushchev, all of a sudden and without any provocation, resume his cursing and swearing at Aref. As I have said, Khrushchev's heart was full of rancor, and when rancor dominates a person he becomes extremely dangerous. Aref did not become ruffled or angry at the continuous insults poured upon him by Khrushchev, but it caused us all a great deal of embarrassment since it was happening in our country.

Khrushchev's behavior led me to avoid him, for I did not wish to come into contact with his foul mouth and vulgar expressions. Despite this, I could not escape the lashing of his tongue entirely. As we were eating a delicious meal of fish, I heard him say: "I will call Sadat 'Gasbadinaxata' "—a Russian word meaning comrade. Then Khrushchev added that the Russians also used the word as a curse. There seemed to be no way I could escape his tongue, and he frequently revealed his hatred of me.

There was another clash after we had invited Khrushchev to address the National Assembly, of which I was at that time the Speaker. Khrushchev was received very warmly and given a standing ovation by the members, and when the session was over we moved to the president's room. The atmosphere encouraged us to set aside formalities and continue our talks as friends. I tried to break the wall of ice created by Khrushchev's behavior at Aswan by making a joke at the expense of Andrei Gretschko, the former defense minister of the USSR, who was also present. I told them: "I have decided to arrest Gretschko and keep him as a hostage here in Egypt until you agree to give us the arms we have been asking for."

Everybody in the room laughed, with the sole exception of Khrushchev. His face had turned yellowish, and he smiled faintly. I fully expected him to fire back with an obscenity from the same filthy dictionary he had used at Aswan. But something forced him to swallow his answer. He looked as though he would choke, and his face was consumed by rancor. Khrushchev laughed only at his own jokes, even if they upset everyone else around.

But despite what I have just said about him, one must admit that the man tried to introduce a more mature system of transferring power in the Soviet Union. In our private meetings, I remember well how Khrushchev used to tell us about Stalin's behavior and his abuse of his power and authority—how Stalin invited all his aides to his apartments every night, got them drunk with vodka till they lost consciousness, and then ordered them to dance before him until after midnight. The only thing that kept changing at these parties were the faces of the people who attended. Each night, the participants would find that at least one or two of them had disappeared or had been wiped out. But no one ever dared to show any sign of curiosity over what could possibly have happened to their disappearing friends. Khrushchev told us he used to say farewell to his wife every time he was called to one of Stalin's vodka and dancing parties. He said he felt as though he were heading for the execution chamber instead of Stalin's home.

The only one who managed to stay close to Stalin for very long was Aleksei Kosygin, and Khrushchev used to make fun of this, asking Kosygin in public: "How could Kosygin remain with Stalin for thirteen years while nobody else lasted more than thirteen months?" It was quite obvious that jokes of this sort were among the important factors that caused Kosygin to turn against Khrushchev and support the plot to overthrow him.

In all sincerity, though, I must pay tribute to Khrushchev

for trying to lay down a system whereby power in the Soviet Union might be transferred in a more civilized manner, in a way that prevented strong men from seizing power by plots—as the case had always been in the Soviet Union. Khrushchev himself never concealed the reality and told us of things that happened in his own country without any sign of inhibition, embarrassment, or sensitivity. For instance, he recalled in great detail how the new leadership after Stalin had succeeded in purging the Secret Police chief, Beria.

It seemed Beria had gathered a great deal of evidence, supported by both photographs and tape recordings, indicating the wrongdoings and deviations of all the Soviet leadership. "It was not possible to arrest or kill him," Khrushchev told us, "for his eyes were present and his spies were monitoring each move and registering every single move or step. At last it was decided to call the Central Committee's Political Bureau to convene for a normal session. Beria attended in his capacity as a member of the Politburo," Khrushchev went on. "The members of the Politburo gathered around the conference table and the door was closed behind them. At a signal, they all got up and went directly to where Beria was sitting, took hold of his neck and kept wringing it until he died."

That was the only possible way they could find to purge Beria. Khrushchev then abruptly altered the course of the conversation, looked at us and said: "You could also apply the same method to get rid of the Egyptian Beria." Khrushchev meant our colleague Zakaria Mohieddin, the minister of the interior, who had been responsible for hunting down the Communists in the country, arresting them and keeping a close watch on their activities. Khrushchev called him an American agent, and his suggestion was that we should call a meeting of the Revolutionary Command Council and in the course of the meeting should seize Mohieddin's neck and squeeze it firmly until he had breathed his last. The Egyptian Communists, said Khrushchev, would then be left in peace.

We in fact discovered when we got rid of the Soviet-backed power centers in 1971 that they were already applying Beria's techniques of "controlling" the population. They liked to boast they had something against each and every Egyptian, and for this reason I determined to get rid of these power centers when the Russian advisers were expelled from Egypt. Some held the view that a committee should be formed to listen to the tapes on which the power centers had recorded the secrets of our citizens, on the grounds that we might find something of use to national security. But I rejected this suggestion and ordered that the tapes be burned, along with their countless scandals and secrets.

To return finally to Khrushchev: rancor had been eating out his heart for many years, and eventually it destroyed him. My own personal experiences bear this out and go back to 1960, when I led a parliamentary delegation to Moscow to discuss our military needs. During this conference over the supply of arms, Khrushchev once more took us by surprise when he abruptly started to lecture us about communism, its achievements, its inevitability, and its triumphs.

He talked of "socialism" like a self-styled great teacher, and when I told him we had socialism in our country, that only made him ruffled and angry. He exclaimed: "Your socialism is one of 'foule' [horsebeans] while ours is one of shish kebab, and you can judge for yourself the great difference between foule and shish kebab." From all these experiences I conclude I would not be exaggerating if I said Khrushchev really hated me. He simply could never forget our past differences, and up until the last meeting I had with him, he remained as he had always been with me: aloof, angry, and rancorous.

The Rancor of Nikita Khrushchev · 59

When the Soviet leaders had become more favorably inclined toward us, they agreed to receive me in Moscow on October 11, 1971. For months I had been trying to impress upon the Soviets the need to negotiate an agreement to supply us with the essential arms for the war I was planning. In typical Soviet fashion, they had pleaded inability to receive me on the pretext that all the Soviet leaders moved to the Crimea during the summer months and would be far from Moscow. I waited until I heard they had returned from their long vacation and applied to them once again. Finally, the answer came, and I left for my visit on October 10.

When I arrived at the airport in Moscow, I was overjoyed to find that Podgorny had not come to meet me. He was the third member of the collective leadership at that time, and I could not stand the sight of him. He had gone to Iran to represent his country at the festivities to mark that country's twenty-five hundredth anniversary. I thanked God for his absence and for being spared the ordeal of having to sit and talk with him. I was met instead by the other two members of the collective leadership, Brezhnev and Kosygin—although the term "collective leadership" invented by the Soviets was simply an illusion. There was no "collective leadership." There was a single ruler: Brezhnev.

Podgorny and Kosygin were completely powerless. Kosygin had since died and lay far removed from their so-called "collective leadership." The question was: where was Podgorny? He was not dead but nobody knew his whereabouts. One day he was head of the whole Soviet Union, the next he had suddenly disappeared. Who could tell where he was or what had become of him? Maybe he was in Siberia, or working as a railway station master, disposed of in the same way as Malenkov. Maybe they had made him a caretaker in a primary school or an elevator operator in one of the government buildings. Nothing is unlikely in the Soviet Union. We had two sessions of talks during that visit to Moscow, among the stormiest as well as the most important I have held with the Soviet leaders. In the course of these talks I came to know them in their true colors.

Taking part on the Soviet side were Brezhnev, Kosygin, Marshal Andrei Grechko, the defense minister, and a man called Panamarov, a carbon copy of Podgorny, with a rigid, inflexible mind and impossible to deal with. Panamarov was, and still is, in charge of the Communist parties throughout the Middle East. He often heads large Soviet delegations on visits to Baghdad, Damascus, or Aden, and has frequently visited us in Cairo.

Not long before, he had come to see me in Egypt when the Sudanese President, Jaafar el-Numeiri, crushed the Communist revolution there in July 1971. I received him at Sidi Abdel Rahman and seized the opportunity to talk to him about our mutual problems, hoping that on his return he would persuade his leaders to change the stance they had adopted toward me. Panamarov listened without taking in a single word I was saying. For he had not come to solve Egypt's problems. He had come to ask me to intervene in order to prevent the execution of their number one agent in Sudan, known as el-Shafi'. "We hope you will ask your friend Numeiri not to execute el-Shafi'," he said. I was well aware that el-Shafi' was one of the most dangerous men in the Sudanese Communist party. Nevertheless, I phoned Numeiri from Sidi Abdel Rahman and said: "The Soviet Union hopes you won't execute el-Shafi'. They have asked me to intervene on their behalf. What do you think?" Numeiri answered: "I would have accepted your intervention most willingly, but it has come too late. It would have been possible to grant your request had you called earlier. El-Shafi' was executed an hour and a half ago."

The news of the execution came as a great blow to Panamarov. He returned home saddened and angry. As for all I had told him about our need for weapons for the forthcoming war, he had taken in not a word. For he had been in one world, I in another. The same thing happened when we resumed our talks in Moscow with the Soviet leaders. As I said, they appeared in their true colors, betraying their real intentions. I began to reassess our relations with the Soviet Union from that moment, in the light of what had been revealed. This led directly to the expulsion of fifteen thousand Russian military experts from Egypt in July 1972.

In my view, nationalism is closely related to patriotism, and because of this belief I have made many enemies in both the Eastern and Western blocs. At one time, the Soviets believed I was an American agent; at another, the Americans thought I was a Soviet agent. The truth of the matter is that I am a full-hearted Egyptian, interested in serving my own country's interests.

I recall two incidents in particular: the first when the non-aligned movement was founded, which enraged the American secretary of state, John Foster Dulles. In his view, each country could adopt only one stance and support either the East or the West. I had criticized Dulles for this attitude, emphasizing the right of each state to choose its own stance. Dulles did not like this at all and began to call me a Soviet agent. Later, when King Faisal of Saudi Arabia came to Egypt following a trip to the United States, he gave Nasser a report from Dulles's brother, the head of the CIA, which stated that Anwar el-Sadat was the number one Soviet agent in Egypt.

Nasser passed the report to me, saying, "Look Anwar, how the Americans view you."

Nowadays, there is not one single Marxist radio station that does not still consider me the number one agent of the United States. Such accusations do not bother me in the least. I know I am the number one agent in the service of Egypt. I am prepared to extend the hand of friendship to the United States or to the Soviet leadership, provided they show respect for the people of Egypt.

·6·

KING FAISAL, A MAN OF DIGNITY

Early in 1973, I took Qadaffi with me—as he had asked me to do—on my way to Saudi Arabia to make the *'umra* pilgrimage, prior to attending the Islamic conference in Lahore, Pakistan. We went to Riyadh and met King Faisal. I had a long-standing acquaintance with him and knew King Faisal to be an honest and upright man, the ideal of Arab wisdom in its sublimest form. Our session with him lasted three-quarters of an hour.

King Faisal was distinguished by a very powerful memory. He had a wonderful ability to quote details, including dates and places, and to describe the condition of those to whom he spoke. He had that nomadic perspicacity. When recounting an incident or conversation that had taken place thirty or forty years earlier, he would tell you, for example, that so and so used to sit fourth to the left; he used to wear such and such; Ali Allouba Pasha's opinion was this; Mahmoud Fahmy Nokrashi's was that, and I answered him thus to the letter.

To sit with King Faisal was to sit with a man who had begun his political life at the age of thirteen, for his father had pushed him into the international sphere of politics at a very early age. From politics he learned honesty, a rare quality, and rarer still, he learned to be straightforward and upright.

In those forty-five minutes with Faisal, Qadaffi listened to an exposé of the Palestinian issue, the like of which he had never heard before. For King Faisal was a walking encyclopedia containing the minutest of details. He spoke from personal experience. He had been a part of everything he recounted and narrated. Faisal thus participated in the recording of history just as he shared in the making of it.

One of the historic facts revealed by King Faisal for the first time was that the English had at one point proposed to the Palestinians that they agree to the immigration of only fifty thousand Jews, in return for which the English would hand Palestine over to the Palestinian administration. The Palestinians at that time said "no." They were supported in this by the Arabs who, in the sphere of politics, know no other word and thus complicate the problem rather than solve it—or perhaps they do not want a solution. Had the Palestinians agreed to that proposal, they would have saved the Arab nation a lot of trouble, anxiety, blood, disaster, and men. Fifty thousand in the midst of those millions are not frightening. They could be contained and would not constitute a threat to the Arab nation.

Thus King Faisal, apart from being a historic figure, and one who had participated in the recording of Arab history, also had an objective outlook and a capacity for seeing into the future. Most unfortunately, Muammar al-Qadaffi did not understand the lesson.

My relationship with King Faisal was one of love and respect. Furthermore, my long experience with him confirmed that what he said, he carried out. His word was law and not subject to discussion. Even in the days of the Yemen War, when a basic difference existed between the two states, my ties with King Faisal were not severed. Thus, until his death in March 1975, my strong relationship with him remained one of brotherhood and friendship.

Many of King Faisal's stands were proof of his nobility and chivalry, in the face of which one could not but love and respect him. In the Khartoum Conference, held in the summer of 1967, Gamal Abdel Nasser met King Faisal, who was accused at that time of being the ultimate reactionary. Faisal had not rejoiced at Nasser's defeat. On the contrary, a stand was adopted that astonished Gamal Abdel Nasser himself; Saudi Arabia, Kuwait, and Libya had resolved to give aid to Egypt, the amount of which was equivalent to the revenue of the Suez Canal. Gamal Abdel Nasser had not imagined that the aid would exceed 5 million pounds, or 10 million at most. That had been the opinion, at that time, of the late Prince Abdullah el-Salem of Kuwait, who had tried to convince Faisal of his point of view. Everyone, especially Nasser who had been defeated, was therefore astonished when King Faisal announced at the meeting that Saudi Arabia would pay 50 million pounds and asked Kuwait to pay 55 million!

My personal friendship with the king began when I visited Riyadh to attend the first Islamic Conference, which was held in 1955. At that time he was crown prince, and Saudi Arabia, Egypt, and Pakistan were the founders of the conference. In spite of the Yemen War, we remained friends, for the meaning of the friendship was the same to him as it was to me.

King Faisal was a man of few words, but when he spoke his words were worth their weight in gold or diamonds. Those who knew Faisal as I did knew that life had taught him many, many things. His political experience and his association with international figures had taught him to be gentle and patient as well as to find an excuse for every human being. Perhaps he had come upon all this when he sat face to face with Gamal

Abdel Nasser in Sudan. For he was before a giant of an Arab leader, but one who had been deeply wounded; he was before the harshest and fiercest of his enemies, but the situation warranted that he hold out his hand toward the wounded commander. Such were the qualities of the noble Arab. King Faisal was of that caliber of men whom one could not but love and respect.

Just as he stood by Gamal Abdel Nasser in his ordeal, so King Faisal supported me in my troubles with the Soviets. In 1971, my problem with the Soviet Union had become greater and more complex. That year, the Communist centers of power were dissolved; then there had been our stand with respect to the Sudanese revolution. Each of those two had involved disagreements with the Soviet leaders, who felt that the regime in Egypt was no longer subject to them. Their every action was proof of their veiled enmity. Consequently I lost all hope in the Soviet Union and its leaders.

I contacted King Faisal and said to him: "You have Lightning fighter bombers?" "Yes, I have," he replied in his brotherly spirit. My problem with the Soviets had always been that their planes were short-range whereas those of the West, including those of English make, were long-range. For the Soviet Union always wished us to remain suspended in midair, never supplying any weapon that could determine the war. When I contacted Faisal and told him I needed English planes, he said: "You are welcome to them. I shall send you twenty of those planes."

But that make of British plane was old and outdated. It had been used in Saudi Arabia and Kuwait. The English had stopped manufacturing them, for they were complicated and excessively costly. The English themselves were content to use American Phantoms.

This was in 1971, the year in which I made two visits to

the Soviet Union, one in March, the other in October, after our relations with the Soviets had greatly deteriorated. This had happened for two reasons. The first was my dissolution of the centers of power in May of that same year; the second was my support of Numeiri against the Communist revolution that took place in Sudan in July 1971 and which subsequently failed. The Soviets had asked me to recognize the new government headed by Hashem el-'Ata. I not only refused, but I also told the Soviet ambassador that I would not countenance the establishment of a Marxist regime on my borders.

The Soviets were very bitter about my attitude toward the July revolution in Sudan. Relations deteriorated rapidly. They resorted to their well-known tactic, that of halting their arms supply. They even stopped supplying me with spare parts for the weapons we already had. That, of course, was apart from their refusal to give us long-range planes. After a lot of argument and trouble, the Soviet leaders allowed me to travel to their country on October 11. As I said, I had previously asked King Faisal for Lightning planes, even though that model was outdated and its maintenance was so complicated that the English themselves had complained about it. Its one advantage was its long-range. King Faisal and I had, as usual, no written agreement. With King Faisal, one's word was enough.

On October 10, one day before my departure, I was surprised to receive a cable from King Faisal informing me that Saudi Arabia had resolved to supply us immediately with twenty Lightning planes. When I received the cable, I laughed; the assistants who were with me had not understood the point of the cable. They had known for some time that we had agreed upon the twenty planes. So why had Faisal now sent that cable? I told them: "This cable is proof that King Faisal is a very shrewd and wise politician as well as one with nobility and values. He wished to help me confront the Soviet. He wanted me to announce officially that I shall receive twenty planes from Saudi Arabia."

It was so . . . When I informed the Soviets, they were furious. The news fell upon the three leaders, Podgorny, Brezhnev, and Kosygin, like a thunderbolt. Brezhnev in particular looked as if he had been bitten by a serpent. They said: "How can you accept planes from Saudi Arabia, knowing what that country represents to the Soviet?" I said to Brezhnev: "My voice has become hoarse from the number of times I and Nasser before me have asked you for long-range planes, but to no avail. We told you we did not want the planes in order to attack, but rather so that we could have defensive weapons with which to retaliate if Israel should attack us in depth. So if Saudi Arabia comes along offering us those planes, should we refuse?"

Shortly before the October War, in August 1973 to be precise, the first Supreme Council of the joint Egyptian and Syrian armed forces met in Alexandria to prepare, arrange and equip for the war that had been set for October. However, Field Marshal Ahmed Ismail, may he rest in peace, saw that the Syrians were backing out, on the pretext that they had not assimilated the new weapons. Those weapons had been with them for over a year, and the Syrians had been trained to use them. We, on the other hand, had received the same weapons very shortly before the war, yet our armed forces had been able to assimilate them fully and expeditiously.

The most important of those weapons was the BMB which had been named "the moving citadel" or the "armed battle car." It had all the characteristics of a tank but carried a greater number of soldiers. In 1972, after I had expelled the Soviet experts, the Soviet Union had showered Syria with weapons, to the extent that Assad had told me he could no longer find any space to store them and had been compelled to use some of the schools as depots for the weapons during the summer holidays. If we return to the October War, we find that fifteen days earlier, Israel had carried out raids on those very schools.

The danger of postponing the date set for the war in October was that it would mean postponing it indefinitely. For from November until spring, the Golan Heights were unsuitable for military action and, when spring came, the Syrians might find another excuse, and so on. For this reason, upon being informed of the attitude of the Syrian command, I told Ahmed Ismail that I would go to Syria to meet Hafez al-Assad. I also asked to pay a two-day visit to Saudi Arabia and Qatar. I did this for two reasons: to inform King Faisal and Sheikh Khalifa that the war was imminent, and to give Ahmed Ismail time to end the Alexandria Conference and to send the Syrian command back to Syria, for I wished the Syrian minister of defense to be in Damascus during my visit there.

A long discussion took place between King Faisal and myself during my visit to him toward the end of August 1973. I said to him: "God willing, we shall wage war against Israel. I have agreed upon this with President Hafez al-Assad." King Faisal raised his face to the sky and prayed to God that we be victorious. Then he said: "Mr. President, this Hafez al-Assad is first of all a Baathist and second an Elouiite. How can you enter with him upon war and feel secure?" For a quarter of an hour I tried to reassure King Faisal about Hafez al-Assad. He was silent for some time and then asked: "What is the role required of me?" I said: "I ask for nothing other than that you take your stand toward a war that will determine the destiny of the Arab nation in all the coming generations." He said: "I have one request. If you wage war, do not cease fire after a few hours or days. Let it be a long battle, for if it is prolonged, we shall be able to take a unified Arab stand."

I shall never forget that phrase. It was one that revealed

the utmost political wisdom. For the establishment of unified Arab stand implied that the whole Arab nation would join in the battle. The Arab nation would not do so unless it was proved that, after the Arabs had lost confidence in themselves, we were in fact able to wage a long war against Israel. This would not come about except after a prolonged war and the passage of some time. Faisal was right, for had the battles not continued, the oil weapon would not have become a factor in the war. We all recall that oil did not become a factor in the war until ten days after it had started. Had we carried out the demand of the Elouiite Baath to cease fire after only forty-eight hours from the start of the war, no victory would have been won and oil would not have been introduced as a weapon.

Another important matter is that in that meeting, which lasted over an hour, King Faisal did not ask me about zero hour. Here is my reply to those who justify their stand with respect to Camp David—which they did not read—by saying that I had not informed them. In spite of the length of the discussion, Faisal did not ask me about zero hour. He knew, without being told, that zero hour concerned Assad and myself alone. I could not mention it, not because I distrusted him, but rather because of military considerations. For this reason, King Faisal was unique and outstanding among the Arab leaders who had been refined by time and experience, and before time and experience by nobility and truth; for what can time and experience do for a person with no nobility, no truth, and no morals?

Some people thought I had asked King Faisal to help us by using oil as a weapon. That was not true. All I said to King Faisal was that it was my responsibility to activate the situation militarily and to fight. "As for your role," I said, "I leave that to you. Do what you can and what you see fit." I told him,

"You are the head of the household, and it is the head of the household who best knows who and what it contains."

Faisal did not need me to say any more. He was a wise man and came to that decision through his own political sagacity, astuteness, and experience. Faisal was the hero of the oil war. The Arab oil was the soul of Western civilization. He knew full well that it was possible for the Arabs to destroy that soul. For this reason, King Faisal's stand at the head of the oil countries and their historical resolution to place an embargo on oil was as critical as a military battle.

In the wake of the October War, King Faisal came to Cairo. Together we visited the Suez Canal and the sites in which the most honorable Arab battle had been fought. In spite of his poor health, Faisal insisted on crossing to the east bank of the Canal on foot. His joy at the victory had made him forget everything else. At the top of the site of the Barlev line, which our forces had destroyed, a moving historic discussion took place between King Faisal and myself. I said to him: "We have now crossed the Suez Canal on foot as you promised. We shall never forget, and neither shall the Egyptian people, your support in every step that realized victory and restored pride and dignity to the Arabs. We pray God that he restore your health so that, God willing, we may together complete the battle."

Faisal replied: "What the Kingdom of Saudi Arabia did was but its national duty toward its sister Egypt and toward the Arab nation. What I now see before me is a miracle for the whole Arab nation. We shall stand by you at all times." Upon our return to Cairo, King Faisal's joy at the victory was very apparent on his face and was revealed in his every word and action.

I still see that man before me; his quiet words still ring in my ears. His death was a great loss to me, to Saudi Arabia and to the Arab nation at large. The bullets that were fired at him left a wound that will never heal in the body of the Saudi Arabian family and the entire Arab nation, especially as the criminal was from the royal family itself. Immediately upon hearing the sad news, I left for the Kingdom of Saudi Arabia. For the loss was a personal one. I had lost a dear brother and noble friend. He was my biggest aid in all situations and the greatest ally in the struggle for our mutual welfare and for the victory of the Arab nation.

What is a human being but a representative of truth and commitment? King Faisal was a man who knew the meaning of morality, of friendship, of dignity, of honor. He was a man to whom I said: "You promised and were true. You pledged and honored your pledge." I said that to him during his lifetime and I say it today after his death, recalling in all pride, acknowledgment, and love a man who was a human being in the role he played, and that is the greatest thing that can be said of a man.

Arrival of the Shah of Iran, 1980. In forcing the shah to leave, "the Western leaders did not realize that they were installing a time bomb inside Iran. They did not grasp what they had done until after it exploded, with its shrapnel raining all over Iran."

One of Sadat's last press interviews. Of the Ayatollah Khomeini he asks: "How can we accept as head of state a sheikh who wears a turban and makes a god of himself? When Khomeini stands up and says his oppression and terror are an Islamic revolution, we [Islamic countries] should oppose him and tell him that he does not represent Islam."

During the October War, 1973, Sadat walks with his wife, Jihan, dressed in a nurse's uniform, at Tahra Palace. "What did that war achieve for us? It taught us that we could gain less by war than by peace."

With King Faisal of Saudi Arabia, 1971. "An honest and upright man, the ideal of Arab wisdom in its sublimest form . . . a man who knew the meaning of morality, of friendship, of dignity, of honor. He was a man to whom I said: 'You promised and were true. You pledged and honored your pledge.'"

Greeting President Assad of Syria and Colonel Qadaffi of Libya. "Qadaffi is the embodiment of the personality known as Dr. Jekyll and Mr. Hyde . . . He has the mentality of a small child. The tragedy is that the toys he plays with are real weapons."

Bidding farewell to Soviet President Podgorny, 1971. "Where was Podgorny now? One day he was head of the whole Soviet Union, the next he had suddenly disappeared. Maybe he was in Siberia, or working as a railway station master. Maybe they had made him a caretaker in a primary school or an elevator operator in one of the government buildings. Nothing is unlikely in the Soviet Union."

With President Tito of Yugoslavia, 1971. "He would often scoff at the empty Soviet slogans, using an amusing catch phrase, always repeating in his delightful English accent, 'Socialism, socialism . . . and *no food!*' "

President Nixon's visit to Egypt, 1974. "Nixon is, and will remain, one of the most brilliant and intelligent politicians I have met in my life." Of President Reagan, Sadat writes: "An easy man to get on with . . . He thinks in headlines and not in details, but is clear in his thoughts, decisions, and answers."

A telephone conversation with President Carter, 1980. "For Carter to have been faced with the enmity of the Zionists and the Israelis is understandable. What is not understandable is the antagonism of the Arabs toward the only American president who had called for a national homeland for the Palestinian people."

Handshake after signing the peace treaty: "It would surely be said [of Sadat's trip to Jerusalem in 1977] that it was an uncalculated gamble. How can you venture to go to your enemies? Are you sure they wouldn't shoot you on the streets of Jerusalem? My answer was ready. This is my fate. The day of my death is set beforehand by God. It might take place in Jerusalem or even in Cairo. The hour is coming, have no doubt."

· 7 ·

MY LOVE FOR GAMAL ABDEL NASSER

In this world, there are two circumstances in which no man can escape from his ego. These are war and imprisonment. In Cell 54, I confronted my ego. We were together day and night, for the loneliness was terrible and that was the only way I could escape it. I did indeed live with my ego, but in spite of this, I was never able to reach it completely. It was as if something stood between us—a darkness from which I had long suffered, but which I had not fully recognized, for I was unable to expose it to light.

When we were allowed books, magazines, and newspapers in prison, I turned to them devouringly, discovering something new in every line I read, something that opened up horizons I had never previously known. My vast readings not only broadened my mental and emotional scope, but they also helped me to become better acquainted with my ego. I managed to overcome a nervous disorder that had been troubling me for some time and which had been brought about by my arrest at 2:00 A.M. in the bitter cold of the winters of both 1942 and 1946.

I did not know the nature of this disorder but sensed it taking its toll of my spiritual well-being. After I was imprisoned and began to live in isolation, the problem rose to the surface. One week in prison is enough to do just that.

Thanks to an article written by an American psychologist, I managed to overcome this disorder. The theme of the article, which was the result of twenty-four years of experimentation by the psychologist, was that a human being is apt, at any stage in his life, to experience a shock that may give rise to a sense of being closed in, as if in a prison to which there is no door. The first door to this prison is to know the cause of the trouble; the second door is faith. What is meant by faith? It is to look upon any painful experience as destiny that must be confronted and borne. Only afterward can the effects of such an experience be overcome. One must not think that there is no solution to a particular problem, for the solution is always there. What is to make you believe this? Your faith that God has brought you into this world for a purpose. The God who created you cannot be evil. On the contrary, He is very good—not at all tyrannical and awful as sometimes depicted. The ideal relationship between man and God is not founded on fear or on reward and punishment. It is built on a value more noble than any other—truth. For mercy, justice, and love are among the qualities of the Creator. He is almighty, for He is the Source of all things. If you take Him as a friend, He will bestow peace upon you, for whatever the circumstances, you love Him and He loves you.

Not only did the psychologist's analysis help me to overcome my nervous disorder, but it also revealed in me an infinite capacity for love in my relationship with creation. This capacity had lain dormant in the vast ocean of my daily life, to be awakened by the trials and tribulations of prison. As of then, love became the chief springboard of all my actions and feelings. Because of this, and because I was so full of conviction and calm, I did not for one moment falter in the midst of the turbulent events that accompanied every stage of my life. Love never once forsook me—it invariably prevailed at the end.

That is the story of my relationship with Gamal Abdel Nasser, or at least one aspect of it. In the eighteen years I was with him, there were moments when I could not understand him or account for some of his actions. Nevertheless, my feelings toward him remained unaltered. They were feelings of love and love alone.

Some have wondered in perplexity how it is that I spent such a long period with Nasser without falling out with him as did his other colleagues. Equally baffled, a foreign journalist in London finally concluded that I had been either of absolutely no consequence or so cunning that I managed to avoid quarreling with Nasser. Of all the men of the revolution, I was the only one who had remained untouched. In fact, upon Nasser's death, I was the only vice president of the Republic.

If the naïve perplexity of those people is proof of anything, it is simply proof of their ignorance of my nature. For I was neither inconsequential during Nasser's lifetime nor shy or cunning at any point in mine. The matter is quite simple. Nasser and I became friends at the age of nineteen. Then came the revolution. He became president of the Republic. I was glad, for the friend I trusted had become president and that made me happy. I felt exactly the same way when Nasser became a hallowed leader of the Arab nation. At times we would differ, and then we would become estranged, sometimes for two months or even more. This would be due either to our differences of opinion or to the machinations of those with influence on him, for Nasser had a natural tendency to lend an ear to gossip.

Regardless of the matter, I never once put myself in a

position of defense. It was not in my nature to do this, whether in my dealings with Nasser or with others. No matter how long it lasted, our estrangement would of course be put to an end when Nasser would telephone me, asking where I had been all that time, and why I had not been in touch with him. I would reply that I had assumed him to be busy and had therefore preferred to leave him to his work. Then we would see each other as though nothing had occurred. This happened many times, but whatever Nasser's actions, they would always be met with sincere love on my part.

At the end of 1942, Nasser took over the Free Officers' Association. Under his leadership and in the span of six years, the organization made great headway. During that period, I was in and out of various prisons and detention camps. When I left prison, I felt an urgent need to return to the army and join Nasser and his colleagues. I wished to contribute to the efforts I had helped to start and which they had continued after me. This I did in 1950 when I returned to the army.

The military bulletin announced that, as of January 15, 1950, I was to return to the armed forces with the rank of captain—the same rank I had when I left. In the period that I had been away, my colleagues in the army had twice been promoted, first to the rank of major then to that of colonel.

The first to pay me a visit of congratulations was Gamal Abdel Nasser accompanied by Abdel Hakim Amer. I learned from Nasser that the Free Officers' Association had grown, gaining in power by the day. As though to prove this to me, or perhaps to put this power to the test, Nasser asked me to sit for the promotion examinations in order to obtain the promotions that had passed me by while I was out of the army. He told me to ignore the difficulties that I would encounter for regardless of their nature the organization would help me. This is indeed what happened. In a short time, I was given the rank of colonel.

Nasser asked me not to undertake any obvious political activity, for due to my history of struggle, it was only natural that I would be watched. This, however, did not prevent Nasser from revealing to me the list of supporters in the different army units. I would visit them and talk to them, but the conversation was always casual, bearing no relation to politics. For, in accordance with the regulations of the organization, I was not supposed to reveal myself or allow them to suspect that I knew they were among the Free Officers.

This was a fundamental principle laid down by Nasser the day he took over the organization, following my arrest in the summer of 1942. The make-up of each unit was to be a secret known only to its members.

My second-in-command before I was arrested had been Abdel Moneim Raouf, who had kept contact with Sheikh Hassan al-Banna, the head of the Moslem Brotherhood. Sheikh Hassan al-Banna had been in total agreement with me that the Free Officers' Association should be independent of any other organization or party, for its aim was to serve Egypt as a whole rather than a particular group.

When I entered the detention camp, Nasser was still in the Sudan. He was sent down with his battalion toward the end of 1942. As soon as he returned to Egypt, Abdel Moneim Raouf was in touch with him in order to draw him into the organization. For Nasser was an outstanding officer, and that had been one of the criteria I had set: that no one be included in the organization unless he excelled in his work in the armed forces. After all, an outstanding officer was in a position of trust and was easily followed by others. Nasser responded immediately. After that, it was not difficult for Nasser to remove Abdel Moneim Raouf and to take over the leadership of the organization himself.

Nasser's leadership of the Free Officers' Association differed from mine. He created secret units in the army, each unknown to the other. The numbers increased daily until the organization included members in the entire armed forces, especially sensitive departments such as the army administration.

In 1951, Nasser felt the organization had attained maturity and required a particular kind of leadership. Many of the members had begun to wonder about the leader or leaders of the organization. At that time, there were five secret organizations in Egypt: the Political Police, the Criminal Investigations, the Army Intelligence, the British Intelligence as well as the American CIA, which had come to Egypt after World War II; these were in addition to another organization controlled by the king and directly responsible to the palace.

Great care was therefore required in the formation of the Constituent Committee. Nasser began to select the members from among those he had known personally in the Palestinian War, those who were his friends and those who had been the original leaders of the organization before he took over.

Nasser's choice of me might seem to be proof of his loyalty. It is true that I had founded the Free Officers' Association, but I had been away for eight years, from the time of my removal from the army in 1942 until my return in 1950. Nasser did not rank among those who are motivated by their feelings toward others, unless those feelings stemmed from a very firm friendship such as his with Abdel Hakim Amer.

Even though we had become acquainted at the early age

of nineteen, I cannot say that our relationship was anything other than one of mutual respect and trust. It was certainly not one of friendship. It was not easy for Nasser to establish a relationship of friendship in the true sense of the word, for he was the eternal doubter, cautious, full of bitterness, high-strung. I do not mean to divest Nasser of the element of loyalty in his choice of me as a member of the Constituent Committee. However, I add to this another element, that of intelligence. From my conduct in the armed forces as well as his knowledge, ever since the early age at which we met, that I was a man of principles and ethics, it was not difficult for Nasser to realize that he could depend on me, and that his act of loyalty in selecting me would make me, in turn, loyal to him for life.

There can be no doubt that Nasser, who was by nature cautious, was fully confident that I would stand by him. I represented a force with experience and history behind it, a power which would support him in the struggle that began in the Constituent Committee even before the revolution. Because of this, Nasser would hasten to me whenever I would return to Cairo, describing the difficulties he was encountering with some of the members. I recall those far-off days. I do not exaggerate when I say that Nasser would spend five whole days of every one of my holidays with me, and those holidays were never more than a week.

We would, on each occasion, examine the position of the organization and the difficulties and problems that confronted us. Nasser had great respect for my experience. In 1951, for example, it was proposed to him that the revolution begin with a series of widespread assassinations. Nasser asked for my opinion. I replied: "Wrong, Gamal. What would be the result? Where would it lead us? The effort expended on the assassinations would be equal to that exerted on the revolution itself. Let us take the direct and honorable road. Let our immediate goal be the revolution."

Then came the 1952 revolution in which I took part. My participation was not in itself a matter of importance to me. Of more import than anything else was the fact that the revolution had been carried out. The dream that had taken hold of my life ever since I was a child of barely twelve years had come true.

It is that which made me live with Nasser for eighteen years without strife. For I wanted nothing. I had no demands of any kind, no matter what my position, whether as a member of the Revolutionary Council, or secretary of the Islamic Conference, or editor-in-chief of the newspaper *al-Goumhouria*, or Deputy Speaker of the National Assembly, or even Speaker of the National Assembly. My love for Nasser never changed; my feelings toward him never altered. I was by his side whether in victory or in defeat. Maybe that is what made Nasser look around him after eighteen years and wake up to the fact that there was one person with whom he had never once fallen out.

I lived with Nasser forever in his debt. For I shall never forget that he drew me into the Free Officers' Association upon my return to the army, after I had been away for eight years—a period spent in prisons and detention camps. I am not like some of Nasser's colleagues who accused him of ruling Egypt like Lord Cromer, or who rose to heights during his lifetime. I bore the responsibility, announcing that I had been responsible for every decision taken by Nasser during his rule.

That is why I said that love conquers at the end. It was not easy for the film over Nasser's eyes to be removed, while deep inside he was full of contradictions known only to God. It is my duty as a friend not to reveal them, but they were there. Nasser died without having enjoyed his life as others did, for it was spent in one fit of agitation following another. He was eaten up with anxiety, doubting every man in advance. The natural consequence was that Nasser left behind him an awful legacy of rancor, whether among the associates closest to him or at all levels within the country itself. It is for this reason that some of those who were wronged gave vent to their bitterness after his death, accusing him of feathering his nest. I testify, as do all those who knew him well, that Nasser was wholly innocent of that charge.

As I said and still reiterate, love conquered at the end . . . this love born of bitterness and pain in Cell 54. There is nothing like suffering to burnish the spirit, removing the rust from it and revealing its true metal. I discovered that I had a natural inclination toward good. Love is the real motive behind my every action. In fact, without love I cannot function.

Most people are impressed by outward success, by social standing, by the money or power they attain. If, for one reason or another, this image changes, they are shaken and break down. They do not know resistance, for they know nothing of honesty with oneself or with others. To them, the end justifies the means.

As for myself, I grew up to believe that the image of myself in my own eyes was more important than my image in the eyes of others. To me, the presidency of the Republic is not of greater consequence than Anwar el-Sadat. Whatever the situation, Anwar el-Sadat is the same: a man with no personal demands. And he who is in need of nothing is his own master.

A few weeks before his death, I visited with President Nasser and he was talking to me about the process of transferring power, both world-wide but especially at home. It seemed evident that Nasser was not feeling at ease about this issue and was worrying about what would happen when his time came to go. He looked as though he sensed his own time was near, and his worry and concern had become acute.

He had been greatly impressed by what happened in Great Britain in the summer of 1970, when the ruling Labor party was defeated in the elections and the queen called upon the opposition Conservative party to form a new Cabinet. "Look, Anwar," he said, "only a few simple words were exchanged and power was transferred from one party to another. There was no fuss, no political crisis, no military coup d'état, no convulsion or clamor." This is the usual process in mature countries, but in immature states the process is entirely different, and the people usually have to suffer a great deal each time there is a transfer of power.

While we were talking about this, it did not cross my mind that Egypt would soon experience a similar transfer of power. In fact it happened in the very same month. We both shared the same fears about what might happen in Egypt after Nasser's departure. Nasser concurred with me that great burdens were awaiting his successor, and I laughed and told him: "Allah will have to help the poor fellow." Strangely enough, I had been convinced for a long time that I was going to die before Nasser. Even more strangely, Nasser thought so as well and had promised to take care of my children after my death. This was after the heart attack I had about that time. It certainly never crossed our minds that Nasser would die in that very same month, or that I would be taking over in a new process of transferring power. But that was the will of Allah.

Nasser was afraid of a group of high officials who wanted power to pass to the Marxists, but fortunately their plot failed.

At the time, I held the post of the one and only vice president and was naturally entitled to assume full responsibility following the announcement of Nasser's death. But poisonous snakes made an attempt to move against me as soon as the announcement came on the radio. Nasser died on a Monday and I had a violent struggle with them from Monday through Thursday evening, as they and their Marxist friends sought to take over the country.*

---

*Editor's note: This refers to the Ali Sabri clique which attempted to topple Sadat and take over Egypt in September 1970.

· 8 ·

NASSER'S DEATH AND MY RELATIONS WITH TITO

Nasser died on September 28, 1970. That day, U.S. President Richard Nixon was in the Mediterranean, visiting his Sixth Fleet, which was engaged in large-scale maneuvers. Relations between Egypt and the United States were very strained at that period, reflecting the hatred that had grown up since our defeat of June 1967. Egypt accused the U.S. of backing Israel with arms; the U.S. believed Egypt had fallen prey to the Soviet Union and had become a threat to U.S. interests in the region. The American newspapers were filled with material that Egypt considered antagonistic and improper.

Nixon's visit to the Sixth Fleet amounted to nothing more or less than a display of force. No one was planning to attack U.S. interests in the Mediterranean. On the contrary: following its great victory over the Arab armies and its occupation of vast tracks of Arab land, Israel, America's principal ally in the region, was experiencing its most successful years, and America shared in its happiness and rejoicing. The United States was prepared to threaten action, right up to a third world war, against any country which threatened the security of Israel.

The nations of the Arab world were, in contrast, undergoing

Nasser's Death and My Relations with Tito · 85

the worst moment in their history, having suffered a harsh defeat that was intolerable to its people. They had to bear the derision of the whole world, which mocked them for having failed to defeat a little state whose population was smaller than one medium-sized Arab capital!

We in Egypt suffered the most pain, grief, and bitterness. The largest and most powerful of the Arab states, we had suffered the greatest disaster in our history, ancient or modern. More painful than the derision of our enemies was the glee of our friends, whose malice only made the disaster worse. The Egyptian citizen no longer believed a word about the war; he had lost all hope in the slogans he had echoed or the victories he had anticipated. Suddenly, we seemed to have become orphans.

On that day, with the U.S. President aboard his flagship and the U.S. Fleet close to our shores, the American newspapers declared that the purpose of the maneuvers "is for Nasser to hear the sound of our guns." It was an extreme provocation and showed the utmost contempt for the feelings of Egyptians, who had still not recovered from the horrors that had overtaken them. But before the roar and thunder of the guns that America wished Nasser to hear had begun, a messenger came to Nixon with an item of news written in a single line. "Nasser died an hour ago," it read.

Nixon did not immediately believe the news. When Golda Meir, the Israeli prime minister, heard that Nasser had died, she too refused to believe it. "Stop this nonsense," she ordered the messenger who brought the tidings. But the news was true. Confirmation poured in from all sides. Whispers of Nasser's death had begun at 7:00 P.M., but we made no official announcement until 11, when I broadcast the news on television myself. It was minutes before the Sixth Fleet's biggest maneuvers were about to begin, but without hesitation Nixon ordered them canceled out of respect for the Egyptian leader. He decided instead to fly direct to Belgrade, bringing forward by one day his visit to President Tito of Yugoslavia.

Taken up by this visit, President Tito was unable to come to Cairo to attend the funeral of his dear friend, Gamal Abdel Nasser. I cannot deny I was taken aback by Tito's attitude. I had expected him to ask Nixon to postpone his visit so that he could bid his friend a last farewell. This would not have caused Tito any embarrassment, since Nixon had already canceled the entire naval maneuvers out of respect for our late leader.

Tito's failure to attend Nasser's funeral truly distressed me. I was bewildered by his conduct, particularly as we remembered the extent of Nasser's love for him and the strong bonds of friendship that had united them for many long years. It was no secret that Nasser was a keen personal admirer of Tito and had been greatly influenced by the Yugoslav president's long struggle to bring happiness to his people and freedom to his country. One effect of this was Nasser's adoption of Yugoslavia's unique party system, the Socialists' Union, in which Tito had combined all the political parties under the leadership of the Communist party. Nasser had proceeded likewise, making the National Union a modified version of Yugoslavia's political system.

So little was Nasser's regard for Tito a secret to the people of Egypt that every time Tito came on a visit to Cairo they would say: "I wonder what will happen in Egypt at the end of *this* visit?" The general feeling was that nothing was adopted in Egypt without Tito having first been asked for his opinion and guidance. For all these reasons, I repeat that I could not see any justification whatsoever for Tito's absence from Nasser's funeral, not a single excuse. It was his one action that I could neither understand nor accept. It was in such contrast to his usual conduct. Many a time he had taken stands I shall never forget; they could only have come from one of the great leaders of the world.

One such stand that inevitably springs to mind was Tito's visit to Egypt two months after the defeat of 1967. There had been no need for him to come, nothing that called for a meeting between Tito and Nasser. Nevertheless he came, giving no specific reason. Boarding his cruiser *Ghaleb*, he headed for Alexandria, where we were overjoyed to meet him. Torn apart by the pain and shattered by our defeat, we had felt we were alone in the world, surrounded by people who hated us. Tito's arrival had a magical effect on us. I was sitting at home in the village of Mit Abul-Kom, thinking of the disaster that had overtaken us, when suddenly Tito came in, like a father, an older brother, a dear friend come to share in my distress, to console me, to ease my pain, to encourage me, to succor me. I said to my companions: "That man has unwittingly done for us what no one else had done; for we were each like a man who had lost his clothes and stood shivering from cold and embarrassment when Tito arrived carrying all the garments in the world."

I was baffled by Tito. In 1967 he came as a genuine human being who knew how to honor his friends—a mass of emotions, akin to us people of the East. On Nasser's death he appeared in a different light, putting the interests of his country above all emotional or personal considerations. Even so, his earlier visit made me love that man and I shall always speak well of him.

I still have unforgettable memories of that visit in 1967. We held a series of talks with him at the Ras El Tin Palace, two delegations facing each other across the long conference table, I seated at Nasser's right, Tito opposite us. Nasser began to speak, expressing his intense anger at the difficulties he was having with the Soviets over rebuilding our defeated army. I recall looking at Nasser's arm and noticing in alarm that it had turned yellow. I was aware that our defeat had aggravated Nasser's diabetes, which he had previously been able to keep under control. After the defeat of June 5, medication failed to keep the diabetes in check and serious complications had ensued. Although his daily dose of insulin injections had been doubled, it was a few months before the amount of sugar in his body was under control.

I was therefore concerned for his health as he spoke of his problems to Tito. The Soviets had halted their arms supplies, saying those they had already sent would take three years for us to learn how to use. We trained our officers and soldiers to use them in five months and asked for further supplies. Nasser told Tito we were in dire need of them to establish our line of defense from Port Said to the Suez, but the Soviets had sent their inevitable reply: "We are unable to answer you as all our leaders have left for the Crimea"!

Nasser's agitation deepened as he said to Tito: "I beg of you, go to Moscow immediately and repeat to the Soviet leaders what you have heard from us. Tell them that we are so displeased that surrender to Israel or the United States would be preferable and less crushing than their treatment of us." Nasser said this to Tito in a fit of rage and frustration, but Tito did not fail to carry out our request. He sailed home and then flew to Moscow where the Soviet leaders heard him out (although they did nothing until the beginning of the following year).

I cite this as evidence of President Tito's nature as a leader and a friend, adopting our cause and fervently advocating it. Tito told us we were not the only ones to suffer from the Soviets. He himself had waged fierce battles against Stalin, refusing to be a Soviet satellite. He did not lose courage. He did not retreat or submit. On the contrary, he drew strength from the people who stood behind him. Stalin did his best to get rid of Tito, pursuing the most base, contemptible and brutal methods. He was behind a number of attempts to assassinate Tito. "Stalin did not leave a single method untried in his attempts to assassinate me," Tito told us. "He even attempted, on more than one occasion, to put poison in my food."

Tito related that story to us as we sat with him at dinner at the Officers' Club in Zamalek in the early days of the Egyptian revolution. To our astonishment, he had brought along his own cook, who had prepared a meal for him different from the one we had offered. We were not used to dealing with rulers and heads of state and were ignorant of such matters. He explained that after he had discovered Stalin's plots to poison him, he had resolved to eat only from the food prepared by his trusted private cook and served from behind his chair by a Yugoslav servant.

Tito informed us that all heads of state followed the same procedure and advised us to emulate his example. We laughed at the suggestion and never for a moment considered assigning a special cook and servant. Not long afterward, however, we discovered a plot to poison Nasser's food. His enemies had bought off one of the Groppi waiters, who had put poison on Nasser's plate at a reception he attended. The plot was discovered at the last moment, and as of that day Nasser decided to take Tito's advice: he would eat only the food prepared for him by his personal cook. And that is what I too now do.

We met with Tito on many occasions. He always opened up to us, speaking of his problems, his dreams, and his opinions of world events. He told us at length of his differences with the Soviet Union and would often scoff at the empty Soviet slogans, using an amusing catch phrase, always repeating in his delightful English accent: "Socialism, socialism . . . and no food." This criticism of the mistakes in the application of socialism confirms my impression of Tito's strength and self-assurance. This is not making too much of him, for he merits the status of a world leader. During World War II he stood side by side with heroes like Churchill, Eisenhower, and De Gaulle, although Yugoslavia is only a small country with a scant population and inconsiderable wealth. It does not produce arms. It does not have an enormous army. Yet in spite of this the Yugoslav people were able, under Tito's leadership, to terrify Hitler's Germany.

These are the qualities of world leadership. And what Tito achieved in war, he also achieved in peace. Stalin emerged from the war victorious and mighty. He was able to swallow up almost a half of Europe and impose Marxism forcibly upon its people. But Stalin, for all his power and tyranny, could not get rid of Tito, even by assassination. Through its armed forces and organizations such as Comicon, the Soviet Union continued to rule eastern Europe according to a specific policy, distributing different roles to each country in order to preserve Soviet hegemony. The Soviet Union specifies to each country what it should plant, manufacture, buy, export, and import. It also determines the production of raw materials and their distribution, all according to a comprehensive plan. But Tito would not accept this *modus operandi*. He would not agree that his role should be limited to carrying out Moscow's instructions, unable to modify or refuse them. It was his opinion—which he repeated again and again to the Moscow leadership—that each country knows its own needs better than anyone else, and that each government should therefore be left to establish economic policy that suits it best. Tito wanted to give absolute priority to the production of food. For it was not reasonable to neglect agriculture in order to give more importance to the production of, say, iron and steel. It was from this that he derived his phrase: "Socialism, socialism . . . and no food."

Tito found no ears in Moscow ready to harken to him. On the contrary, he had to listen to criticisms of his style of rule. So he decided to act independently, knowing full well that the other eastern European leaders thought as he did, even if they did not share his boldness. He planned his own agricultural policy regardless of the fact that it clashed with the Soviet master plan. Not only that, but he decided to challenge the Soviet theory itself where it concerned agriculture. For Tito was convinced that the peasant could not be nationalized. He believed the greatest of all the Soviet Union's mistakes was to deprive the peasants of the tenure of the land. Instead of tending his own farm, the Soviet peasant simply carries out instructions from a high-ranking official, and for this reason Soviet farm production is very meager.

The agricultural slump in the Soviet Union happened in other Communist countries, even Yugoslavia, where Tito was taken by surprise to find that production was insufficient to feed his people. He found himself forced to import foodstuffs from abroad to avoid a frightful famine. This was happening in spite of Yugoslavia's excellent soil. Throughout history, the Yugoslav people had been self-sufficient, the farmers irrigating and harvesting the land they owned in order to increase their income. When the land was nationalized, all incentive for increased production was lost, and the nationalized peasant was offered only the minimum of his sweat and labor. Agricultural produce dwindled. Tito decided he could no longer stand and watch the disaster, as other Communist leaders had done. Completely ignoring the laws of Soviet hegemony, he passed his own law allowing the farmer land tenure up to a limit of twenty-five acres.

This bold decree worked a miracle. The Yugoslav peasant regained his freedom, production increased, modern methods of farming were introduced, and the country not only fed its own people but also exported food to numerous other countries in western Europe. Tito disregarded the storm that his decree provoked in Moscow, and the Kremlin leaders were finally impelled to accept his policies. With all its power and authority, the Soviet Union stood powerless before the leader of a small country who wished only to provide his people with enough food. Tito's victory proved that the Communist theory of agriculture is the cause of the veiled famine suffered in many countries where it has been imposed by force. There is more proof of this in the fearful shortage of farm produce inside the Soviet Union itself.

Tito proved his leadership and boldness with this act of defiance. His courage is characteristic of true world leadership. Khrushchev also had many reservations about Marxist theory but was not as courageous as Tito and so only said secretly what others said openly. I recall how surprised we were to hear Khrushchev say to us on one of his visits to Cairo: "Listen, folks, I beg you not to repeat what I am about to tell you, for if it reaches the ears of the Politburo I shall be swiftly dismissed from office." We laughed and Khrushchev laughed with us before he went on to say: "If the wheel of time could be turned back and I had the power, we would not have nationalized either housing or crafts or craftsmen." These had all rapidly proved a failure, but in spite of Khrushchev's convictions and in spite of his influence and power, he could not find Tito's courage to speak his opinion and do something about it. This is the difference between one leader and another.

The leaders of another east European Communist country—Czechoslovakia—were like Khrushchev and lacked Tito's courage. During a visit to Prague, I sat next to a friend who had a high-ranking position in the leadership of the Czech Communist party. When he was assured we were alone, he confessed to me that the nationalization of housing, crafts, and agricultural land had created problems to which there was no solution. But he could not find the courage to proclaim his views and rectify the errors.

True world leadership needs special qualities that are only available to the strong and courageous. Tito had those qualities, and they earned him the hatred of the Soviet leadership that stooped to undermine him by any means in its power.

I recall for example when Nasser and I, at the end of an official visit to the Soviet Union, agreed to stop over in Belgrade for two days to meet President Tito before returning to Cairo. A few moments before we boarded the plane at the Moscow airport, a high-ranking official who had once worked for *Pravda* in Cairo said to Nasser in a mocking tone, full of resentment: "Ah, you are on your way to visit the Communist Emperor!" It was a phrase used by the Soviet leaders to denigrate Tito whenever they could. Because Tito liked to live in palaces built by former princes and kings, they pretended he lived in a style different from the rest of the Communist leaders. But Tito's only mistake was to do publicly what they did secretly. For the leaders of the Soviet Union—at the summit of communism, holding Marxist views and supposedly protecting Socialist peoples—live the life of American millionaires! The only difference between them and Tito is that Tito did not conceal his movements or forbid the publication of pictures taken in the government palaces where he resided. The Soviet leaders reside in emperors' palaces in the Crimea, elegant chalets are reserved for them on the shores of enchanting lakes—and they do not permit photographs or one word to appear on this capitalist life-style they enjoy at the expense of the people. How unjust of them, therefore, to dub Tito "the Emperor of Communism"!

I knew Tito well and can say he was distinguished by rare qualities and a nobility that made you respect him, admire him and be influenced by him. I was most careful to keep him acquainted with our military and political situation when I took over the reins of government in Egypt.

Tito took a truly honorable stand as the appointed time for the October War drew near in 1973. I had made preparations to ensure there would be a unified Arab stand when the life-and-death battle began. Then I prepared the way for African support and, following that, for international support. That left only the nonaligned countries to deal with. Luckily, I met Tito in Algiers at the Nonaligned Conference of September 1973, only a few weeks before the battle. I admitted that war with Israel was imminent and that, in fact, the date had been set. Tito wished us success and did not ask me about zero hour nor press me with questions.

I returned to Cairo and a few weeks later the whole world was awakened to news of the sweeping Egyptian attack. After six hours of fighting, I was surprised to receive a request for a cease-fire from the Soviet ambassador, who said it had been asked for by Syria. Of course I refused this absurd request, but the reason for it soon became evident. From the first, the situation on the Syrian-Israeli front was not favorable to the Syrians, and Moscow's great fear was that Syria might be lost and its regime—which they had shored up after their dismissal from Egypt—might be irretrievably overthrown.

At this juncture, Brezhnev phoned Tito and said to him: "Please intervene with your friend Sadat and persuade him to agree to the request for a cease-fire or he will be the cause of a complete Arab debacle. Syria faces the danger of a sweeping defeat and el-Assad has asked us three times already to arrange a cease-fire, but Sadat still refuses." Tito heard Brezhnev out, but he was never in touch with me to inform me of Brezhnev's request. I heard of it only when I later visited him in Belgrade. He told me Brezhnev had used a not too polite word to describe me, which caused Tito to flare up and answer: "Sadat knows what he is doing and is better able than anyone to assess the situation. I cannot intervene to ask him to do something he does not wish to do. If you want to inform him of your opinion, it is for you to contact him from Moscow."

Later in the war, Tito took an even more noble stand on our behalf. The battle was at its fiercest; Egypt had lost 500 tanks, Israel 1,000, and Syria had lost 1,200 tanks in a single day. We were in great need of replacements. I found none but Tito to ask for help. We asked for 100 tanks, or one armored brigade under the system we use. Tito, without delay, sent us 140 tanks, ready for immediate action. All were supplied with ammunition and their fuel tanks were filled up. He asked for no advance payment, as arms dealers do, and the tanks were transported directly by train to the front. It was an astounding action, and after the disengagement I decided to fly to Belgrade to thank him. What increased my respect for him was that he had sent the tanks to a country the Soviet Union had told him would be utterly defeated! For Brezhnev had assured him Israel would destroy us within days if not hours.

After that I always made a point of visiting Tito every time I returned from Europe or the United States. Once I also asked the Egyptian Vice President, Husni Mubarak, to visit Belgrade after one of his trips, and he duly cabled to ask for an appointment with Tito. The reply came that the appointment was with Tito's deputy, and not Tito himself. Mubarak immediately canceled the visit and I approved of his action, telling him: "From now on, leave the man alone. We will not attempt to impose on him."

Later, when Tito toured the Gulf states but did not visit Cairo, I was not offended but understood that he had to keep his distance so as not to impair his economic ties with the "boys" who ruled Libya.

Yugoslavia has enormous interests in Libya, and Tito depended greatly on their oil. To anger the child Qadaffi could deal a hard blow to the Yugoslav economy. For these reasons I was not angered by Tito's stand in the period before his death, which followed Arab rejection of Egypt and its leadership. The organizers of the rejection were like children behaving foolishly, and Tito knew them to be foolish. He knew full well that I would appreciate his position and understand his every step, although others would view his actions differently. Our feelings toward him were of gratitude and loyalty.

· 9 ·

MY PEACE INITIATIVE

When I am faced with a problem, no matter how impossible a solution might seem, I am careful to avoid losing my temper and flaring up. More importantly, I do not limit myself to finding one solution to a problem but consider it essential to look for alternative solutions; so if the first fails, I can move on to the second, then to the third, and so on.

I have learned that purity of intention is very helpful in creating an atmosphere conducive to the solution of the most difficult and complex issues. This is what happened when I began to think of how to solve the most difficult and complex problem we face: the Arab-Israeli conflict. It is true that a comprehensive solution to the problem has not yet been reached, but it is equally true that we have been able to take a first step in the direction of that just and comprehensive solution we seek.

The beginning was not easy . . .

It all started when Jimmy Carter invited me to visit him in February 1977—just one month after he had taken over as president of the United States. The problem posed by the Arab-Israeli conflict was the basis of our talks in Washington. The agenda consisted of three items:

Item 1: The problem of the Arab lands occupied after the 1967 War.

Item 2: Relations between the Arabs and Israelis.

Item 3: The Palestinian question, which we considered the basis of all the other problems.

I myself had added a fourth item to the agenda: namely, the situation in Lebanon. Civil war had broken out there, with many implications.

We did not differ greatly in our discussions over the first item concerning the Arab territory occupied after the 1967 War. We differed, however, over the second. This emerged when I said to Carter: "How can you ask us to have normal relations with the Israelis while they continue to occupy our lands? Israel is anxious to normalize relations before a withdrawal agreement is reached, in order to justify the occupation and its continuation—just as they once used Israeli security as a pretext to occupy the lands of others. The October War gave the lie to the theory of Israeli security. Because of this, they have come up with a new excuse: their call to establish normal relations with the Arabs before they agree to withdraw."

I also said to Carter: "It is unacceptable for the Israelis to call upon us to normalize relations before we agree to end the occupation and draw up a timetable specifying the stages of a complete Israeli withdrawal from Arab lands. To talk of normalizing relations while the Israeli occupation of our lands continues is unacceptable to any Arab thinker."

We discussed that item at length. Carter was unable to convince me of his point of view. But the visit was nevertheless a very important one, for we pledged to work together toward solving the Arab-Israeli conflict, no matter what difficulties this created. I remember my words to Carter: "We shall never lose hope. We shall certainly find a solution to each problem we are faced with. What is important is that we maintain direct contact between the two of us, so that we can exchange points of view on every step we take." Carter was sincere in his pledge. He wanted to participate in the search for a just and comprehensive solution, acceptable to all parties.

It is enough that he was the first American president to call unceasingly for the right of the Palestinian people to a national homeland. No American president before Carter had dared to voice such a view. Carter alone stood up courageously, expressing his opinion firmly. He promptly incurred the hatred and wrath of world Zionism, which did everything in its power to destroy him. For Carter to have been faced with the enmity of the Zionists and the Israelis is understandable. What is not understandable is the antagonism of the Arabs toward the only American president who had called for a national homeland for the Palestinian people. No one else had given a thought to this, from the days of Harry Truman, in whose term the Israeli state was first created, right down to the time when Carter took over the U.S. government.

I remember the time Crown Prince Fahd of Saudi Arabia went to Washington and said to Carter: "Rest assured. Yasser Arafat has agreed to accept the Security Council resolution number 242" (which recognizes the right of Israel to exist as a state within secure frontiers). Fahd added: "Here is Arafat's signature on this written document, testifying to this." The very next day, Yasser Arafat stood up and announced that he did not recognize resolution 242 and that he had not spoken with Prince Fahd on the matter. Prince Fahd was infuriated. As soon as he returned to Saudi Arabia he issued a violent condemnation of the Palestine Liberation Organization, in which he referred to the signature on the document. He had realized beforehand how he should deal with Arafat and his supporters. Unfortunately, I never followed that procedure in my own dealings with Arafat. The PLO people would sit with me and approve issues and resolutions, but as soon as I announced them, they would evasively deny they had anything to do with them.

Carter received the same treatment from the Syrians. They baffled and bewildered him, wearing him out. At the beginning, they agreed with Carter that the Arabs should go as one delegation to deal with the Israelis, instead of in separate groups. Carter asked for my opinion. Knowing the political maneuvers to which the Syrians are addicted, I rejected the proposal, saying to Carter: "One delegation will achieve nothing. The conference will be transformed into an auction for never-ending slogans."

After that, everything came to a standstill as a result of Syria's insistence on its demand. After a while, Carter was in touch with me again and tried to persuade me to accept the Syrian point of view. He said to me: "It will be to the Palestinians' advantage if the Arabs go as one delegation. In that way the Palestinians will be represented. Israel won't object to the presence of a Palestinian representative within a single delegation; but if they go as a separate delegation, then they will object." I knew this was another maneuver on the part of the Syrians, but I agreed to Carter's request nonetheless. The Syrian rulers were taken aback. They found themselves in an extremely embarrassing situation. The road to the conference had been paved—but in reality they had no desire to see the conference take place. So they went back on their word, refusing to participate in a single delegation. They began to pose problems as to how the delegation would be chosen, with never-ending objections to everything proposed.

Carter did not know how to handle the Syrians, for these were his first dealings with them. He imagined they would be as good as their word and was taken aback when he found that the word of a Syrian was in fact a thousand and one words, and that what they agreed to one day they rejected the next, returning to it the day after. Carter's bewilderment grew. He found himself at a loss. Taking up his pen, he wrote me a letter in his own hand, sending it to me through an intermediary. Neither the American embassy in Cairo nor the Egyptian embassy in Washington knew anything about the contents of that handwritten message.

In it, Carter confessed his bewilderment at these political maneuvers, whose aims he could not fully understand. He had been working toward a solution of the problem, and he had imagined his efforts alone were enough to secure for him the cooperation and gratitude of all concerned. He had therefore been stunned by the maneuvering, and the complications had left him at a total loss. I answered Carter's letter with an assurance that I was still resolved on what we had pledged to do during my visit to the White House. We would find a solution that would not only get us out of the vicious circle they were forever trying to keep us locked into, but we would also reach a comprehensive solution to the Arab-Israeli conflict. I admit here that when I wrote my reply to Carter I had no ideas in my mind about the shape of that comprehensive solution. All I had were good intentions, coupled with a firm resolve.

I sat down to think. All the possibilities gathered before me. The issue was a major and complex one, requiring in turn a major and complex solution. From the newspapers, I learned that Menachem Begin had won the Israeli elections and, as prime minister, intended to travel to Rumania to meet President Ceausescu. Ceausescu is one of my closest and oldest friends—and was also a friend of President Nasser. He had often pressed Nasser to allow him to take on the role of mediator with the Israelis. His insistence had greatly embarrassed Nasser, who tried to get rid of it by saying: "You go and speak to the Israelis yourself instead of me."

When I took over from Nasser, Ceausescu repeated his proposal to me, advising me to negotiate directly with the Israelis. I excused myself each time with the words: "The time is not yet ripe for such a step." I always made a point of staying with Ceausescu on my visits to Europe. In Rumania, I stayed in a district called Sinaia, which received its name because the king of Rumania once visited St. Catherine's Monastery in the Sinai. He had been impressed and, upon his return, ordered a smaller version of St. Catherine's to be built in a mountainous region that he then called Sinaia. With its green mountains, flowing waters and magnificent views, it is among the most beautiful spots in the world. Each time I visited it, I would stand in awe before the splendor of the Creator who had fashioned such natural beauty, owing nothing to human artifice. Then I would tell Ceausescu in jest: "In the near future, when the Sinai is once again returned to us, I will invite you to the original St. Catherine's."

Thinking about these things, and having read that Begin would visit Rumania soon, the idea of a solution to our problem came to me. I recalled how Begin often challenged the Arabs, saying: "You Arabs have a problem with us. Your lands are in our possession. You have rights that you talk about and are always calling for. How can you regain them without coming to sit with us around the conference table?" This was a question Golda Meir directed to the Arabs, before Begin. It was a question echoed by the world at large. Our image before the world was truly an ugly one. We were calling for our land, but we were refusing to ask it of those who occupied it. We were calling for our rights, but we were refusing to sit down with those who had deprived us of them.

All we did—what the Arabs still do, even now—was to sit in our capitals and issue warnings to Israel and her friends. Every day we would hear an Arab leader threaten the Israeli leaders, calling upon them to return the occupied lands—"or else." Then the Arab leader would direct another warning to America to put pressure on its protégé, Israel—"or else." The world heard those threats and warnings and laughed scornfully at us, making fun of our peculiar methods of obtaining our rights and recovering our occupied land.

We had waged the October War, and God had ordained victory for us. Through this victory, we have proved ourselves and retrieved our confidence in our own abilities. Why not, then, put aside slogans and think anew about how to solve the problem in a modern way that the civilized world could accept and understand? I remembered how Ceausescu had urged me to negotiate with the Israelis. I did not think of him as a mediator, negotiating in our name. I thought of how he had urged us to negotiate directly. I resolved that Egypt should take its problem into its own hands and not leave it in the hands of others. Ceausescu could be of some help to me in that.

Shortly afterward, I boarded the plane for el-Taef to make my first visit to Saudi Arabia. I met my Saudi brothers: King Khaled, Prince Fahd, and other princes. But I did not inform them of another approach to peace that was growing in my mind at that time: the initiative to end the state of hostilities with Israel. At that point, the initiative itself had not finally crystalized. Some time earlier, I had had in mind a plan to call the big five to meet in Jerusalem, in order to guarantee peace and security for both parties in the Middle East conflict.

This was the idea that had concerned me as I flew over the Ararat mountains on my way from Rumania to meet the shah in Iran. But for several reasons I decided then and there not to carry that idea further.

First and foremost was that Brezhnev would be among the big five, and while Brezhnev was a friend and a reasonable man, he was nonetheless tied by a number of political considerations that would have hindered him from taking a positive stand. He was also restricted by the points of view of his Syrian and Palestinian allies. And he could never forget my blow to the Soviet Union in the Middle East (when I decided to expel the Soviet advisers in Egypt). The second reason for abandoning this idea was the position of China. Though China supported the Arab cause completely, I felt she might abstain from coming to the meeting as she did in the Security Council.

The third reason was that some heads of state could have been tied up with their programs, and this could have hindered their movement for six months or more, making it difficult for them to come to Jerusalem on the date I proposed.

For all these reasons, I changed my mind about the form of the initiative while flying over the Ararat mountains. I wanted to prove to the whole world that I was a true man of peace and that I was not calling for an initiative just as a maneuver. This is why I did not inform my Saudi brothers about my plan. When I left Saudi Arabia on my return to Egypt, the idea of the initiative started to take further shape. My thoughts centered around a simple idea: Why should I go round in circles to reach my target? My obvious and only target was peace, and peace cannot be achieved under just any circumstances. It can be achieved only through direct meetings between the parties to the conflict.

I was thinking along the following lines: Why shouldn't I go to the Israelis directly? Why shouldn't I stand before the

Knesset and address the Israelis themselves as well as the whole world, putting forward the Arab cause and stating its dimensions? As I thought about it, I conjured up what the reaction might be to such a move, which no one would expect. It would be said that it was an uncalculated gamble. How can you venture to go to your own enemies? What guarantees do you have? Are you sure they would not shoot you on the streets of Jerusalem as they did before with Count Bernadotte, the chief UN mediator in Palestine?

My answer was ready: This is my fate. No man can escape his fate. The day of my death is set beforehand by God. It might take place in Jerusalem or in Cairo, on a bridge or under a bridge. The hour is coming, have no doubt. How can we forget the words of God almighty: "Wherever you may be, death shall overtake you; even though you be in fortified castles."

At that point, I felt the intellectual strain. Then happiness overwhelmed me—a happiness previously unknown. It is the happiness of a man when he gets hold of the truth after a long and painful search. I made my decision and I never hesitated. On November 19, 1977, witnessed by the whole world, I was moving out of the plane to set foot on Jerusalem's soil. The effect of my initiative was to show the Israelis they were dealing with a new style of Arab leadership. Before I went to Jerusalem the Israeli leadership had been able to mobilize its people against Arab attitudes, and these attitudes had spread to Zionist organizations throughout the world. The Israeli leadership had been able to persuade them there was no hope for peace between Israel and the Arabs and had portrayed the Arabs as monsters who wanted only to drive Israel into the sea. All the slogans ever written in the Egyptian and Arab press were used by the Israelis to perpetuate the idea that there was no hope of security with the Arab world.

This is why the reaction to my peace initiative was so strong inside Israel. The Israelis just could not believe it. Before my initiative, Israel talked peace and made war, while the Arabs talked of war and did nothing. The situation was always volatile as a result. But after the initiative, the Israeli people themselves became a pressure group in favor of peace. They were impressed by this new style of leadership in the Arab world. Sadat's conduct shows that the Arabs are not so bad as we thought they were, they said. And so Israel's public opinion was affected.

If we look back through history we see the horrors brought upon Egypt by war—the martyrs, the destruction, the delays in development. Egypt became a backward country because of the slogan "war is supreme." This is why I opted for peace. I thought that without it Egypt would revert to the old attitudes, and I thought it was important to create an atmosphere that fostered development, so that Egypt could survive and become a partner in the twenty-first century before it was too late.

These were the thoughts that were constantly in my mind during the period between the visit to Jerusalem and the signing of the peace treaty between Egypt and Israel.

Why did I always think we could achieve so much through peace? By a simple calculation: how much war had cost Egypt and the Arab world since 1948. Until the October War, 99 percent of the economic burden was borne by Egypt. Even after the October War, when the entire Arab world made a lot of money out of oil and added to their wealth, Egypt by contrast was drained of its resources. So whenever the Israelis created problems during the peace negotiations, my thoughts would go back to the burden we had to bear, and I would opt for peace.

I also thought of the direct results of the October War.

What did that war achieve for us? We regained a very small portion of the Sinai and we managed to reopen the Suez Canal. Against this we have to set the cost to Egypt of 14 billion pounds, plus all the losses in men and equipment.

We all know that Israel was taken by surprise in the October War. But it also taught us that we could gain less by war than by our peace initiative. In the October War, the United States sided militarily with Israel, and we knew we could not fight the United States. We also know the Soviet Union would never side with an Arab country as the United States did with Israel. These were my thoughts and calculations about the difficulties of embarking on a new war to regain the rest of the Sinai. Such a course would have set us back by more than a century. As a ruler, I felt I had a responsibility before God and my people, even though it would have been easier to act like any other Arab leader and drag my people to destruction while acting as a hero of slogans.

This is why I chose peace and did not drag my country into war. I found I could achieve the same goals through peace.

· 10 ·

EGYPT AND THE ARABS

Egypt has been bitterly attacked in the Arab world for concluding the Camp David agreement with Israel. But the sad truth is that those who attacked us so vehemently did so even before the Camp David accords were known. They attacked an agreement they knew nothing about, even though it could have led to the realization of our Arab goals. They did so simply because we dared to negotiate with the Israeli enemy.

The pattern began even while the negotiations were underway in 1978. At that time, King Hussein of Jordan was in London, staying at the same hotel as one of my aides. The king approached my aide, a comparatively young man, and asked him: "Are you in contact with Sadat?" Hussein then asked him to call me in Camp David and inform me that Jordan was ready to join in the peace process. The young aide was astonished at the king's attitude—Hussein had come to see him secretly in the aide's room—and called me immediately to tell me with enthusiasm of what the king had proposed.

I asked him for King Hussein's telephone number and called him back. At that point an agreement with the Israelis seemed unlikely; so when Hussein asked me how the negotiations were going I told him no progress had been made and the gap between both sides was still very wide. He then asked if there was any hope of success. I told him we would have to wait and see but promised to let him know as soon as we made any progress. I thought it was not wise to include Hussein in the negotiations until we had reached a concrete agreement with the Israelis. To my astonishment, King Hussein was quoted by Barbara Walters on American television next day as saying that Sadat had called him in London and invited him to join the peace talks. The king said he had refused the offer and decided to cut short his journey to Europe and Morocco and return home to Jordan.

I had to ask my aides to make an official denial of the American television report. What Hussein had done was a typical piece of international auctioneering. He called me and offered to join the talks. He then told the Saudis, who issued orders to him to act to the contrary. King Hassan of Morocco acted in the same manner. When the negotiations at Camp David were over, I had planned to head directly for Cairo. But King Hassan insisted that I should stop in Rabat where King Hussein of Jordan was also scheduled to meet me.

After the Camp David accords had been announced, it was clear the entire Arab world had turned against me. So I asked Dr. Ashraf Ghorbal, the Egyptian ambassador in Washington, to inform the Moroccan ambassador that I would prefer not to stop in Rabat so as not to cause any embarrassment to the king. But the king refused to accept my apologies, which were conveyed to him twice. I therefore stopped at Rabat on my way home and met the king. Again, King Hassan took the same course as King Hussein and announced some time later that I had insisted on stopping in Rabat.

Subsequently, I refused to see the Moroccans' former ambassador in Cairo, Abdel Latif el-Erraki, because of the conduct of King Hassan. When the shah was in exile in Morocco, Hassan had sent his ambassador to request that I extend an invitation to the shah to live in Egypt. In exchange, he offered to defend Egypt's position at a forthcoming conference in Baghdad. I then called the shah by telephone in Morocco and offered to fly back with him to Cairo the following week. The shah said he was bewildered at what was happening, because Hassan had just ordered him to leave the country that same week!

What does all this mean? It means only that King Hassan does not know how to take a firm stand. He had urged the shah to live in Morocco in the first place, then asked me to invite him to live in Egypt; and when he thought my invitation was delayed, Hassan immediately issued orders that the shah should leave Rabat in twenty-four hours. That was very strange conduct indeed. For all these reasons, I therefore refused to meet with Hassan's ambassador when he came to Cairo in 1981. He came with a message from the king saying Morocco would restore diplomatic relations with Egypt if we in turn would sever our relations with Israel and renounce the Camp David accords. The envoy returned to Rabat with the message that his mission had been rejected and Sadat had refused to see him. All this has come about because of the Camp David accords. The entire Arab world turned against me after that.

For their part, the Saudis took a relatively moderate stand, although King Khaled both privately and publicly denounced my visit to Jerusalem from the very first day. But I harbored no ill feelings against him since his stand was consistent from the very start. Some other Saudi officials wanted to carry out secret measures against me and met at a camp in the desert to plan their action. But the news was leaked and nothing came from it. Some contacts of course did take place between Egypt and the rest of the Arab world after the Camp David accords. For example, Qadaffi's cousin came to see me on my birthday at my home village. He offered me a reconciliation with Qadaffi on one condition: that it should be kept secret. I replied by saying: "You do not respect the deals you make in public, so how can I respect a secret one?" The Libyan envoy told me Libya was in agreement with the first part of Camp David, which dealt with the peace treaty, but was against the second part, which concerned the future of the Palestinians.

I said this is what I had expected to happen. Yet anyone who read the Camp David accord would find that it did not seek to impose a solution on the Palestinians. All we did at Camp David was to show we wanted to end the Israeli occupation of the West Bank and the Gaza Strip, setting out a transitional period before the Palestinians ruled themselves. Was not such a move better than occupation?

I repeated that we never claimed to speak on behalf of the Palestinians. We told Carter and Begin we could not act on their behalf, but wanted only to end the Israeli occupation. This at any rate is what I told the Libyan envoy. But I am sure Qadaffi would deny it, like Hussein and Hassan did before him.

During the days of the late King Faisal of Saudi Arabia and the late Shah of Iran, we all three dreamed of constructing an oil pipeline to link Suez with Alexandria. This was at the time when the Suez Canal was still closed and just after Israel had built a pipeline linking Eilat to the Mediterranean. Our idea was for a pipeline to bring Iranian oil to the Mediterranean, where it would be carried in turn to Europe. The capital we needed was estimated by foreign experts at $400 million.

I called King Faisal and asked for the money. Faisal said we could borrow the money from Saudi Arabia or pay for it out of our share of the oil revenues, but I told him we would like him to become a partner in our project. Our objective was not just to create a project that would bear fruit for Egypt, but that all the Arab nations should share the benefit of such strategic projects. My aim, I told Faisal, was that the Arabs should think with one mind and move toward one single Arab nation. I always wondered why the others were satisfied by depositing their money only in banks and receiving interest. I thought it would surely be better to invest our money in industrial and commercial construction projects involving the whole Arab world. The model I had in mind was that of the European Economic Community. When King Faisal realized that I was insisting that Saudi Arabia should participate as partners, he said his country together with Kuwait and Qatar would raise 50 percent of the capital and Egypt would have the remaining share. The three Arab countries were very generous and participated immediately. The project succeeded and each country made a 30 percent profit from it.

One of the projects I had contemplated was to exploit our Mediterranean coast for the benefit of our brothers in the Gulf area who suffer from the strains of uncomfortably hot weather. I thought the Mediterranean coast could be divided into free zones and that each country could invest in one of these zones, leading to real economic cooperation among us. Thus the Arab world would be presented to others as a true political and economic power.

Unfortunately Faisal died and Arab relations suddenly deteriorated. It was no longer appropriate to think of economic cooperation instead of the sort of cooperation that is built on sheer slogans.

We also thought the Shah of Iran would welcome our Mediterranean project and invest in one of the free zones. After the 1973 War, the shah had telephoned me and made a similar gesture by investing in the redevelopment of Port Said. I thought an offer of a free zone on the Mediterranean would help to repay this debt. But events in Iran moved too quickly, and before we could make any progress the project was buried under the Iranian revolution.

Sudan was now the only power in the area that was still able to benefit from our scheme. That is why Egypt has made the offer to Sudan of a gift of land on our Mediterranean coast to act as a port for them. I discussed the plan with President Nimeiry and agreed that we would, in effect, be trading off property—so that just as the Sudan would own property in Egypt, so Egypt would be able to own property in the Sudan. This was my initiative, although according to our constitution it had to be approved by the National Assembly.

I thought such a project would lead to true Arab cooperation and always looked forward to creating an even greater project, with a small Saudia, a mini Kuwait, a tiny Qatar, and so forth, on the Mediterranean coast. I am really sorry about the ruptures that have occurred in the Arab world, because before the Arabs launched their campaign against Egypt, I was always thinking of true cooperation along the line I have explained. But the Arabs revealed their true features when they decided to start a boycott of Egypt at their Baghdad summit meeting. So today, the door for cooperation is open only to the Sudan.

·11·

ISRAEL'S HOSTILE ACTIONS

During 1981 Israel embarked on two hostile acts against its neighbors that threatened to disrupt the peace process begun during my visit to Jerusalem. Their planes bombed a nuclear reactor in Iraq, and Israel wreaked vengeance on Lebanon by killing four hundred Lebanese in an air raid and wounding a further thousand. The story has been circulated that we did not take a firm stand against these Israeli actions because we were waiting until April 1982 to recover the Sinai. This view has no basis in fact. The date of the final Israeli evacuation from the Sinai was fixed when we signed the peace treaty with Israel in 1979 and was not negotiable or open to renewed discussion.

We cannot express strongly enough our condemnation of these two Israeli acts. But the two operations differed. Of the two, the more serious was the bombing of the Iraqi nuclear reactor, because its specific aim was to disrupt the peace process. The action of Israel in undertaking this raid renewed old wounds. We thought we had healed these wounds during the preceding three years, but we were wrong. Still more time was needed.

The greatest danger in the situation the raid created is that Israel has resorted to its old ways, which have been rejected by all. One may recall that during my speech to the Knesset in Jerusalem I declared that 75 percent of the problem between the Israelis and the Arabs is the psychological barrier that divides them. In fact, I undertook my mission to Israel to try and break down that barrier before we began with the peace process. The psychological barrier I am talking about arose because of the bitterness that prevailed for thirty years. During that period, we witnessed four wars between the Arabs and the Israelis. Following each war, hatred increased and the psychological barrier grew higher and higher.

I went to Israel and called upon its people to help us break down that barrier. And I can say with confidence that in Egypt this barrier has indeed been overcome since my visit to Jerusalem. Why? Because after the 1973 War we were no longer in need of extending it or allowing it to continue. What I sincerely fear is that Israel's actions will lead to the renewing of this psychological barrier and the reopening of wounds I thought had been healed forever. It is, in fact, a big mistake on Israel's part.

Our attitude toward the peace process was put to the test once before—in 1978, when the Arabs met in Baghdad and severed relations with Egypt, trying to isolate her and force her out of the international organizations. All these attempts failed, and it was clear to all Arabs that there was no alternative to the Egyptian moves and its results. But Israel's bombing of the Iraqi nuclear reactor put Egypt and the peace process to a new test—the peace process in which Israel is a partner.

I have said before, and I still believe it is valid to say again, that no one can shake the basis of the peace process. We succeeded against the Arab challenge by being solidly committed to peace. This should remain our position. Israel committed a grave mistake, a mistake that represents a threat to peace, but we must not allow ourselves to be diverted from our path.

If Israel's objective was to deprive all countries of the Middle East the opportunity of acquiring nuclear reactors—and this, honestly, must be Israel's objective, even if she denies it—then this would be enough to threaten to destroy everything we have worked for. Israel's attempt to possess the sole right of building nuclear reactors and to deny the right to all others only reopens old wounds.

But destroying peace is not an easy thing. I have said many times that the peace process is the only constant factor in an area undergoing many changes. But the Israeli action remains the greatest threat to the peace process we have yet faced.

Only one of the three partners who signed the Camp David accords can upset the peace process: the United States, Egypt, or Israel. And then one of those three—Israel—undertook an irresponsible military operation. The danger is that their operation gives a blank check to the Soviet Union and Syria to renew their agitations against us.

We all know of the lies of the Syrian leader, Hafez al-Assad, we know his conduct in his country, we know what he does to his people, we know what he did to Lebanon and how he is waiting to threaten King Hussein of Jordan. We also know the attitude of the Soviet Union. This superpower does not want peace between two small countries that have been torn by war for the past thirty years; the Soviets are working against peace with the aim of freezing the current situation.

The Soviet Union did not hesitate to say no in the Security Council to peace between Egypt and Israel. For this superpower wants to impose its views on other countries. If a country in the area wants to make peace with another, it has first to obtain the approval of the Soviet Union, for it alone decides who makes peace with whom.

I must warn the Israelis against the blank check they have given to the Syrians and the Soviet Union, for it will lead to the following consequences:

- a blessing on what has happened in Afghanistan, occupied by the Soviet military;
- support of Communist insurgencies in Africa;
- condoning the conduct of the child who rules Libya;
- enclosing ourselves inside an Iron Curtain with Syria, Libya, South Yemen, Algeria, and some Palestinians.

We have to reclaim that blank check and tear it to pieces so it cannot be used. For this, I rely on the solid support of the Egyptian people, who are now facing this horrible test imposed by the Israelis. I call it horrible because it is so. Only three days before the Israeli bombing I sat discussing matters with Prime Minister Begin at Sharm-el-Sheikh and announcing our continued commitment to the peace process. Then three days later I heard that Israeli fighter planes had bombarded the Iraqi nuclear reactor on Begin's orders.

I must admit I found Iraq's reaction to the raid quite objective. I thought they might have accused Sadat of complicity and claimed I must have known of this action during my meeting with Begin. But they reacted in a very responsible manner. Begin announced immediately that he had not informed me of anything at Sharm-el-Sheikh, but he clearly had not considered those who would take advantage of the situation. The Soviet Union quickly accused the United States of having prior knowledge of the operation.

I cannot defend the United States, because I have no idea whether they knew of the operation in advance or not, but I can tell you of certain developments that took place a few hours before Begin made his announcement.

At eight o'clock in the morning, Husni Mubarak, the vice president, received an urgent call from the American chargé d'affaires who asked to meet him immediately. The vice president received him at his home, where the chargé asked if Cairo had been informed of the attack beforehand, during my meeting with Begin at Sharm-el-Sheikh. Mubarak said surely this had not happened and suggested he call President Sadat to confirm it, which he did. Husni Mubarak conveyed to the chargé d'affaires my assurances that I had not been informed beforehand, and I then told him the Israeli action was a big blow to peace.

Now I have something to tell my people: Don't lose hope, don't allow the psychological barrier to rise again. You have expressed your total condemnation of this act, but do not lose hope in peace. I have seen how the Israeli people want peace.

We are facing a severe test, a test of the peace process itself. But I am confident the peace process will achieve its aims and will follow the course we have designed for it.

I give the same advice to the Arabs, but my advice to them follows the advice I have given to my own people, for if my people accept it, the Arabs will follow suit. I only ask the Arabs to abandon emotionalism and allow reason to prevail in these critical moments.

My comments on the Israeli raids into Lebanon fall into a different category. Of course we do not accept haphazard bombing of Palestinians and Lebanese. Not one, not twenty rockets will help to solve the problem of the Palestinian people, but on the other hand we totally reject Israel's conduct.

For our part, we in Egypt would like to tell the PLO man who ordered the firing of the Katiousha rockets that you have to calculate before firing that you are facing Israel which is quite prepared to retaliate.

When we say such things, the other Arabs usually reply that Egypt is not in a position to condemn the PLO attacks because we ourselves undertook such an attack against Israel in 1973.

On that occasion, I have to say, when the United States

intervened to help Israel after seventeen days' fighting in the October War, we calculated that we had to call off our attack. I announced I would not proceed with a war against the United States, for I know the strength of America and I shall never drive my people or my country into such an unbalanced fight.

Could the Palestinian resistance, plus all the Arabs, match Israel's strength today? No. So why then venture on a lost battle? They talk of a cease-fire, but in my opinion this is a loss and a blow to Arab dignity, degrading all our values.

None of this hinders us from saying that what the Israelis did in Lebanon was horrifying. But the Palestinian who ordered the firing of the Katiousha also did a horrifying thing, because he brought all this destruction on his people.

Where is reason, where is right, and where are the calculations in a war? For now we hear that Syria is asking for billions of pounds to leave Lebanon. We all know Lebanon is lost between the Syrians and the PLO, and we all know the Palestinians are lost between Syria and Israel. This is the equation in Lebanon.

I think the remedy for the situation is to resort to a comprehensive peace that guarantees the solution of the Palestinian question. These were the first steps that we agreed upon at Camp David for finding a solution to the Israeli occupation of the West Bank and the Gaza Strip and setting up full autonomous rule there. Israel should withdraw to secure points until the Palestinian people decide, along with the United States, Egypt, Jordan, and Israel, what the next step should be.

I therefore think that the man who took the decision to bomb an Israeli settlement and who was not prepared for retaliation was as responsible for what happened as was Begin. I think the Lebanese and the Palestinians are victims of Israel in the same manner that they are victims of those who ordered the rockets to be fired inside Israel. And they are also the victims of Hafez al-Assad, who entered Lebanon seven years ago pretending to protect the Palestinians, but who has now become the pretext for Israel to move into Lebanon.

So I ask the Arabs: Is there no sound man among you to save you from all this rupture?

· 12 ·

MY RELATIONS WITH BRITAIN

There is a traditional Egyptian saying that deep friendships can sometimes follow enmity. This has been the case in my relations with Great Britain. For many years I was an enemy of the British. I lived as a fugitive from their army of occupation. I was thrown out of the Egyptian army because of the British, I was arrested because of my opposition to them, and I suffered a great deal throughout the British occupation of my country. I never gave in to them nor deviated from my principles. Neither their terror nor the promise of reward could make me surrender.

I thought many times of blowing up the British embassy in Cairo with all its occupants as an act of protest. I saw the embassy as the symbol of our national shame: the seat of the British high commissioner, who was the real ruler of Egypt, above the king, above the government and above the people. But time passes. The British left Egypt long ago. Our revolution was successful, and since then I have been able to develop strong ties with British politicians and, more recently, with the British royal family, including her majesty the queen.

When the queen's husband, Prince Philip, duke of Edinburgh, visited Egypt in 1981, I invited him to lunch at Ismailia. We had a very good time together and spoke about many things, including the forthcoming wedding of the Prince of Wales. Prince Philip told me the wedding day would coincide with the birthday of my wife, Jihan. I was surprised he knew my wife's birthday, but he told me that our two wives—that is the queen and Jihan—had discussed this at a recent meeting. The queen had found this out, and Prince Philip had remembered to tell me of it at Ismailia.

I found Prince Philip to be a man of superior education, a genuine athlete, and a politician of the first order, with long experience. He is polite, gentlemanly, and frank. We discussed the political situation of our turbulent world. I said to him: "Who could have thought that relations between Egypt and Britain could have become so strong?" I added: "I really would like to praise Britain's attitude toward Egypt both before, during, and after the October War of 1973. Britain sold us sophisticated weapons and has helped us to diversify our supplies. Its international policies today are just and positive—in contrast, I may say, to British policies during the occupation, the revolution, and the 1956 Suez War." Prince Philip accepted my praises gracefully.

His visit to Ismailia was followed by a dinner in his honor held by the British ambassador at his residence in Cairo. I wanted the prince, as well as the British government and people, to see that Egypt knows how to return a favor and express its thanks for its support—as well as how to defend its honor against their aggression.

I therefore told the British ambassador by telephone that I would be attending the dinner. The prince and the ambassador were both surprised at my decision, which was contrary to the usual protocol. But I had done it intentionally, so that

Prince Philip and Britain would feel that Egypt and its president had gone out of their way to be courteous.

So, for the first time in my life, I entered the building that had in the past been the bastion of British occupation and conspiracy, but which had now become friendly territory. The reception I received was more than cordial and all formalities were dispensed with.

I moved from room to room in the ambassador's residence and saw there the pictures of all the British ambassadors who had served in Egypt—with one exception. The portrait of Cromer had been removed. I considered that its removal was a very courteous move by the British. It respected my feelings and it showed that the British know better than anyone how Lord Cromer disgraced Egypt when he ruled our country as high commissioner in the early years of this century.

During the dinner I told my hosts that I had once seriously planned to blow up their embassy and all its occupants in protest against the continuation of British occupation. We laughed over that.

Plans for my visit to see President Reagan were laid soon after his election, when Secretary of State Haig came to Cairo with an invitation to talk with the president in Washington. I had arranged my trip for early August 1981 when I heard from Haig that some of my Arab brothers had insisted that they should see President Reagan first. I laughed at their reasoning—the timing was not in the least important. But what was unfortunate was the weight they gave to such trivial matters, which only made them look comical.

In any event, I rescheduled my trip and accepted an invitation from Mrs. Thatcher to call on her in London before I went to Washington. Before my departure, I went as usual in retreat to Mount Sinai to finish my third reading of the

Koran during the last days of the holy month of Ramadan. I broke my fast with the Sheikhs of the Sinai and then visited the village of St. Catherine.

I took all my children and almost all my grandchildren with me on my trip, because it gave me an opportunity to spend time with them—an opportunity I do not often get in Egypt because of the pressure of my work.

In London, we stayed at the Egyptian embassy, and all of us watched a video recording of the wedding of Prince Charles and Lady Diana Spencer.

Next day, Monday August 3, was my meeting with Mrs. Thatcher. But before I left to see her I had an appointment with some photographers from Madame Tussaud's waxwork museum. They had already made one model of me, and I had sent them one of my suits to put on it, but when they sent me a photograph of it I was astonished to see they had made me look exactly like Dracula! Then they told me they had portrayed only what they saw in front of them. Anyhow, they became convinced by my objections and destroyed that first waxwork so that they could make another one.

The working session with Mrs. Thatcher finally started. We were received by a guard of honor outside the Foreign Office, the commander of the guard welcoming us in Arabic, saying in our own language: "The guard is ready for inspection, Mr. President." After that we had a private meeting with Mrs. Thatcher in Downing Street. We spoke of the role that might be played in the Middle East by Europe—and Britain, in particular, as chairman of the EEC that year. I was impressed by Mrs. Thatcher's grasp of every detail, and from the first moment I felt relaxed in my conversations with her. Our views were in agreement, and I can say that a strong friendship started between us during this short meeting.

The same applies to the foreign secretary, Lord Carrington,

who has an easy sense of humor, which he uses to break the ice in getting to know one. He has an aristocratic background, but in our meetings he always deferred to Mrs. Thatcher, the prime minister, who comes from a modest background.

Our meeting concluded with an agreement that Europe should play a more active role and participate with us in the peace process. The Camp David accord does not mean we are seeking only a limited or a separate peace: we are looking for a comprehensive solution to the Arab-Israeli conflict. In the first stages of the peace process the United States played its role alone; in the next stage, Britain and the other Common Market countries must join in.

The next step they can help with is to achieve immediate mutual recognition between Israel and the Palestinians. I explained to Mrs. Thatcher how important it was that Israel and the Palestinians had just agreed on a cease-fire in Lebanon as a first step toward this mutual recognition. I was pleased that Mrs. Thatcher agreed with me—and more pleased that she agreed with me that it was important to build on this move in an attempt to achieve the next step. We agreed that Britain should join in our attempts to achieve our aims. I asked Britain to intensify her consultations with Saudi Arabia on that topic. Our talks ended in complete agreement. Our friendship was cemented.

As we left Downing Street, the press crowded round me and asked how the talks had gone. I told them I always looked forward to my meetings with the "Iron Lady." I also met with James Callaghan, the former prime minister, and talked mostly about the rise of the new party in Britain, the Social Democratic party. Callaghan told me this represented a new trend and that the Social Democrats could become the party of the future.

Next day, I went to visit the queen; it was my second

meeting with her. She had postponed her holiday in Scotland so that she could meet with us. Prince Philip took us into the dining room, but I told the queen I never eat anything during the day, only in the evening. She answered: "I knew this beforehand. We shall serve you only juice." I found a glass of orange juice in front of me. It happens that I can't stand citrus juice because of my gastric stomach, but I had to drink it anyway. But by this time my mind was on my talks with the queen, who takes a broad interest in international affairs, revealing a deep acquaintance with developments in the Middle East.

Afterward, while taking coffee in the drawing room, I invited her to visit Egypt. She welcomed the invitation and said she would like to come as soon as possible.

That same day we crossed the Atlantic to start our visit to President Reagan. I was met at Andrews Air Force Base by Secretary of State Haig. Some might wonder why the president himself did not come out to receive a visiting head of state. The question is a fair one, but it seems the answer lies in U.S. protocol, which does not allow the president to receive foreign guests at the airport. The formal reception is always at the White House. I did not mind this, because I always prefer to have a day of rest after a long journey. So I spent the rest of the day with my children and grandchildren playing around me and laughing in Blair House.

I went to the White House the next day to meet the new president. Because of the oppressive heat and humidity of Washington in the summer, I found myself longing for the cool breezes of our own Alexandria. This may sound strange coming from an Egyptian, used to heat, but the climate in Washington during August is really unbearable. Some people who saw me on television may have noticed that I had to change my suit before I left the White House because I was sweating so profusely.

Before our negotiations began, George Bush, the vice president, whispered to me that he hoped I was not angry about the anti-Sadat demonstrations outside.

"I asked: "Which demonstrations?"

He replied: "Those emotional shouts in Arabic, of which, I'm afraid, I don't understand a word."

I laughed and told him: "But those are my children. They are Egyptians come here to welcome me."

We broke off our meeting and agreed to meet with the president the next day.

I then prepared for a meeting at the State Department. Whenever I go there, I have to confess it brings to my mind the bad memory of John Foster Dulles, the secretary of state under Eisenhower, a man who did so much damage to American-Egyptian relations. I could not get this idea out of my mind as I climbed the steps to the State Department building. Haig opened the meeting by telling his colleagues: "This is a working session. President Sadat is with us. Go ahead and ask him whatever you want." And the questions flowed. As the meeting progressed, a message was brought in for me. It informed me that my youngest daughter, Gehan, had been taken to the hospital with a hemmorhage. You can imagine my feelings as a father.

It was difficult for me to control my emotions in front of this gathering of politicians. But I was forced to continue with the meeting beyond its scheduled time because of the enthusiasm of the participants. I did not say a word to them about what had happened to my daughter. I split my personality between father and statesman. But God knows how worried I was at that moment!

I finally managed to get away from the meeting but had to pause on the steps of the State Department to talk to the press about what had transpired.

Speeding on my way to the hospital, I could think only of my daughter Gehan. I prayed to God for her recovery. I recited some verses from the Koran to comfort me and give me patience. We arrived at the Washington Clinic in record time—the same hospital, incidentally, where President Reagan had been taken after he was shot. I rushed up the steps to my daughter's bedside and found her safe with my wife.

Senator Charles Percy had taken care of all the arrangements. He showed the same gallantry an Egyptian would have done in standing by a friend in need.

Over breakfast the next day, I found President Reagan an easy man to get on with. He understands what goes on in the corridors of power and the backstairs of politics. He thinks in headlines and not in details, but is clear in his thoughts, decisions, and answers.

Later in my trip, I met former President Richard Nixon at the home of the Egyptian head of mission to the United Nations in New York. As always, I found that Nixon followed international developments closely, especially in the Middle East. Nixon is, and will remain, one of the most brilliant and intelligent politicians I have met in my life.

I also met with former President Jimmy Carter and felt how difficult it must have been for him to leave the White House. It made me think of my time in prison and how I used to say: "A strong politician must be there when the people want him, and be prepared to leave immediately when they cease to want him."

Neither a politician nor an actor should stay too long on the stage, but be prepared to withdraw when the right moment comes. For this reason, I would like my people to accept and understand the decision I shall take next year.*

My admiration and esteem for Carter increased after my meeting with him in Plains, Georgia. He had no personal hatred nor remorse over Reagan's victory, and he was prepared to continue to help to push the peace process forward, and to go to Washington at any time to meet Reagan for that purpose.

---

*Editor's note: Sadat had planned to retire in 1982.

· 13 ·

MEMORIES OF WAR

The seeds of our defeat of June 5, 1967, were sown much earlier, during the years of Nasser's autocratic rule. These years made me realize that the mistakes made by a democracy in a whole generation do not compare with the mistakes that can be made by a dictatorship in a single day. When we deprive people of their freedom, all manner of evils can follow, as we have seen recently in Iran.

Twice in my own lifetime I have voted for dictatorship—both occasions on the same day, July 27, 1952, after the revolution that overthrew King Farouk. I did so because I was totally convinced that this was the only way to rid our country of corruption. I am not ashamed to admit that I later changed my mind. The years of autocratic rule that followed the revolution hurt the Egyptian citizen twice over: once through removing his freedom, and again through the practices that were adopted by the committee that was set up to abolish feudalism. This committee wounded the pride of many families whose wealth was confiscated.

All this happened at a time when Arab-Egyptian relations were at their lowest ebb. The Arab world was disunited. In September 1962 Egypt had committed many troops to save the revolution in Yemen and to try and bring that country out of the Middle Ages. Aden was liberated as a direct result of our support. In return, we lost thousands of our young men in the Yemeni hills, thousands of miles away from home. The Yemeni War contributed to the increasing ruptures in the Arab world. Saudi Arabia was against us. Many other countries joined them and took a stand against Egyptian military intervention. Most important, the Yemeni operation forced Egypt to send its elite forces overseas. These forces did not return until after the 1967 War.

We therefore entered the 1967 War against Israel—a fierce enemy, armed to the teeth—with a large part of our army miles away from the front. They were fighting a battle that was not ours in order to defend a revolution that was also not ours. The Yemeni War might have been used as a training ground for our armed forces, but unfortunately this did not happen. We later found that our military leaders there were exploiting the situation in order to feather their own nests. This was revealed after the 1967 defeat during the hearings against Abdel Hakim Amer, who was then commander of the armed forces.

During this period, the Soviets as usual were unhappy to see one of their allies becoming too powerful and were terrified that Nasser's influence would spread from the Atlantic Ocean to the Gulf. His power was beginning to exceed what they wanted. He had become a legend in the Arab world after the nationalization of the Suez Canal and the war of 1956. The Soviets were angry at his growing popularity, and Khrushchev therefore provoked two crises against him. The first was in 1958, the year when Egypt united with Syria, and the second was in 1961 when the union broke apart.

The Soviets attempted to build up a rival to Nasser in order to lessen his popularity in the Arab world. In 1958 they thought Abdul Karim Kassem, then president of Iraq, could be set up as Nasser's rival, but their expectations foundered. Kassem was overthrown and left the scene. They tried again with Salah

Gedeed, a Syrian politician, who showed his loyalty to the Soviets by preaching their Marxist doctrine. Gedeed abolished all titles, calling everyone "Comrade," the form used in Syria to this day.

On a visit to the Soviet Union in May 1967, just before the catastrophe that overtook our armed forces, I met a friend, a Russian politician called Smirnov, one of the deputy foreign ministers. I spoke to him about Gedeed, and he told me of the miracles he had performed. I warned him of their experiences with Abdul Karim Kassem and added: "You learn nothing from your mistakes." Smirnov disagreed, then took me on one side and whispered something in my ear. "You return today to Cairo," he said. "As soon as you arrive, go straight to Abdel Nasser and tell him that we have information confirming the fact that Israel has mobilized ten divisions of troops on the Syrian border." I did not delay one second after my arrival in Cairo. I rushed immediately to Nasser's home to tell him what I had learned from the Russians. Nasser said the Russians already transmitted the same message directly to him. This is typical of the way they act. The story was a lie.

Later, the Russians tried the same tactics with Colonel Qadaffi when they told him in a private message: "Take care. Sadat has sent an armored division from Alexandria to the Libyan border." Qadaffi was afraid and became emotional, shouting to the five continents against me. Only later did he find out the Russian story was not true. Our "armored division" was a mobile bakery for the use of our troops. The Soviets' objective was to dangle Qadaffi upside down by his legs and leave him swaying in the wind.

In the case of the false alarm over the Israeli mobilization against Egypt, this was also just another example of the characteristic tactics of the Soviet Union.

At about the same time that this was going on, Field Marshal Amer had gone to Pakistan, where he heard a lot of critical comment about Egypt's acceptance of the Israeli occupation of Sharm-el-Sheikh. Amer lost his head and sent Nasser a telegram asking him to order the closure of the Tiran Straits, which leads to the port of Sharm-el-Sheikh. When Amer returned to Cairo, Nasser asked him: "Do you know the meaning of your request? It would mean war with Israel. Are you ready for such a war?" Amer answered: "Our forces are ready for anything."

Nasser wanted to stop this Arab auctioneering; so he ordered the mobilization of our forces in the Sinai. As I said before, at that time the bulk of our army was in Yemen. So, one day, the Egyptian people woke up to find rows and rows of tanks and armed vehicles rolling through their cities to the Sinai. A big press campaign was started to stir up the people. A plan had been drawn up for the Sinai mobilization. On Air Force Day, May 22, Nasser made a speech announcing the closure of the Tiran Straits and requesting the United Nations to move its troops away.

Every day I went to briefings at the army headquarters with Nasser, remaining there until midnight. Our last meeting was on June 2, a Friday. By this time, the whole world was living on its nerves. In Jerusalem, the prime minister, Levi Eshkol, trembled at the prospect of war, although Ezer Weizman, the chief of staff, assured him that Israel would win. In Washington, President Johnson called for restraint and the Soviets asked for calm. Messages flew in from all sides.

I must now state something for the historical record. There are eyewitnesses alive today who know the truth of what I am saying. On the night of Friday, June 2, we met at the headquarters of the armed forces, where Nasser, in his capacity as president of the Republic, signed the final plan for war. Then he spoke to the commander of our air force and said: "The first strike will be against our air force." The commander of the air force replied: "We are expecting it, Mr. President. We have based our plans on that expectation." Nasser asked him: "Have you assessed what our losses might be in the first strike?" The commander replied: "It will not exceed ten percent, not by any means."

Then the president spoke to all the commanders present: "It is now Friday night. Yesterday, a new coalition government was formed in Israel. If war is to break out, it will come tomorrow or the day after—or Monday, at the very latest." It appeared as though Nasser was reading from a book. The war broke out on the morning of June 5—Monday.

I swear now before God and the people that the war plan we had agreed upon was never implemented. The unauthorized changes that were made led directly to the fall of al-Arish on the first day of fighting. And the fall of al-Arish meant that the war had ended in favor of the enemy. Al-Arish was the army's forward depot, and it fell without resistance.

On June 5, I woke up to the news that Israel had attacked us. Our radio claimed we had shot down twenty-seven Israeli planes. My only comment was that the Israelis had made a big mistake in attacking us. We were ready for them, and I was confident of victory. I did not rush out and put on my clothes but entered the bathroom to shave and take a shower as I did every morning. Then I told my driver to take me to army headquarters. Above Cairo and the al-Masa airport I saw smoke rising. At first, I was not worried: I knew we had a good network of anti-aircraft missiles and thought the smoke came from the fallen Israeli aircraft.

Soon, I noticed another car beside mine. It carried the Soviet ambassador, and I thought he was on his way to congratulate our government—or that he had been summoned to headquarters to answer a request for more arms and ammunition. I told my driver: "Follow the ambassador's car. He will be going to headquarters." Our two cars drew up outside the headquarters building. I gave the ambassador time to enter before me. When I went in an enthusiastic young officer told me we had now downed fifty Israeli planes. But when I went underground to Amer's office, I found a very different story.

Amer stood behind his desk, his eyes shifting, not concentrating on anything. Two members of the revolutionary council sat silently on a couch. The way Amer looked—his eyes out of focus—and the silence of my colleagues made me anticipate an unexpected catastrophe. I looked at the field marshal and said: "Good morning, Abdel Hakim." He did not answer. Not one word. After a whole minute, he realized I was there and said in a low voice: "Good morning, Anwar." I moved to the couch and asked my colleagues: "What has happened?" The answer was the last thing I expected. With one voice they said: "The Israelis have destroyed our entire air force." One of them added: "Do you remember what happened in the 1956 war when the Israelis destroyed all our planes? They repeated the same strike this morning. We lost all our air force."

The news came as a thunderbolt. I sat stunned, unable to believe what I had just heard! I felt bitter as I fell on a couch in the office, a million questions erupting inside me. We sat in silence. Suddenly the sad silence was broken by the ringing of a telephone; Abdel Hakim answered it. The call was from our forward base at al-Arish and the news it brought was bad—the Israelis were advancing on the base. As military men, we understood at once the meaning of this news: al-Arish, our firmly fortified base, was essential to the defense of Egypt. If it should fall, the war would be over. According to the original plan on which we had agreed, al-Arish could only be reached after bitter fighting and heavy losses for the Israelis. Even if they were prepared to accept such losses, we doubted they could have reached the base.

But we now learned the agreed upon plan had been changed. So to whom could I address my bewildered questions? To whom could I speak? The voice of Abdel Hakim continued to break the silence of the office, still answering the call from al-Arish. Suddenly the door opened from the adjoining salon, and Gamal Abdel Nasser entered.

I had not known that Gamal was at headquarters, although his house was less than two minutes away. He had just been talking with the Soviet ambassador, who had arrived at our headquarters. After a quick greeting, he turned to Abdel Hakim and said: "Abdel Hakim, why did you call for the Russian ambassador?"

Abdel Hakim answered: "I want to ask them to arrange a cease-fire because the United States has entered the war and has destroyed our air force." In front of me and our two colleagues, Nasser said: "Abdel Hakim, the United States has not entered the war. It was Israel and not America who destroyed our air force." Abdel Hakim attempted to talk, but Nasser interrupted him: "I do not agree, and I will not permit the announcement that the United States has entered the war until you bring me the tail off an American aircraft with its insignia."

While he was speaking these words, our radio was claiming we had shot down seventy planes—when in fact all our airfields, including those at Heliopolis and Huckstep, had been hit by the enemy.

An argument ensued between Nasser and Abdel Hakim Amer, in the middle of which Nasser asked us to leave, wanting to be alone with Abdel Hakim to berate him for calling the Russian ambassador. He told me afterward: "This is a political act and has nothing to do with the work of the commander-in-chief. It is in my jurisdiction as president, and if the commander-in-chief wishes to notify the ambassador of anything, he should submit his request to the president of the Republic who should make the decision whether to send for the ambassador or not and whether to ask for a cease-fire or not. This is the work of the president of the Republic."

After we had left, I went upstairs and found Mahmoud Fawzi, chief of staff of the armed forces—and later commander-in-chief—facing me. I asked him: "What is the position of our armed forces in the Sinai after the attack on the air force?" Fawzi replied: "The troops are still holding fast, but the destruction of our air force is a most critical matter." I told him: "You must attempt something," and he replied: "We are doing all we can." It was obvious the man was in a state of shock.

I then took my car and returned home to Giza, where I sat in my office, pondering. The sequence of events passed before my mind: Abdel Hakim's shifting eyes while he spoke to me . . . how he had sent word to the commanders in the Sinai, asking them to meet him at the al-Meliz airport on that fateful Monday, June 5! The commander-in-chief, and with him all the commanders of the armed forces, in a plane in the middle of war! And awaiting them at the al-Meliz airport, the Sinai commanders! Naturally, the Israelis had heard of this, and it presented them with a golden opportunity. The commander-in-chief in a plane, airborne, on a trip. This meant definite instructions had gone out to the Rocket Corps not to launch any rockets until the commander-in-chief's plane had landed.

The Israeli air attack came. Their planes arrived while the Rocket Corps had instructions not to open fire because the commander-in-chief was airborne. They arrived at 8:30 A.M.—the breakfast hour for our pilots after the inspection shifts. Routine had not changed, even though we were on the brink of war and the enemy might take that into account. What happened that day did not reflect Israeli cleverness. Never! Our commander-in-chief had paved the road for them. At one stroke they destroyed our entire air force. Not one rocket was fired!

When the attack came, Abdel Hakim Amer was airborne, midway on his trip. When he realized what was happening he turned back and personally witnessed the bombing of our airports. He continued to circle in the air, his eyes shifting. They were still shifting when I met him in his office at army headquarters. Finally, the commander-in-chief was able to land at the Cairo airport, which had also been hit. The tragedy was at its peak. Almaza Airport and our planes there had been completely destroyed. He was met by the commander of the air force, who reported to him: "All is in order, sir. Our planes have all been hit."

All this went through my mind as I sat at home in Giza. The time came to take a walk on the terrace, but before I did so, I again phoned headquarters and asked Abdel Hakim about our position. He replied: "The battle now centers around al-Arish." I replaced the receiver, stunned, and started pacing the terrace a number of times, the road to the pyramids in front of me. Along the road came trucks from Tahrir Province, carrying the *fellahin* chanting: "To Tel Aviv!" They had heard that on the radio.

My pace quickened as I cried out silently: "To Tel Aviv? It is al-Arish that has fallen. The war is over; the air force destroyed in an hour this morning. In exactly sixty minutes it was all destroyed; as a result it's all over in the Sinai, and in the whole of Egypt, too." My inner voice groaned as the trucks rolled past, the *fellahin* still chanting; "To Tel Aviv!"

"Please God, what shall we tell these people?" I asked myself. "When shall we inform them of the catastrophe? What will be the result of it? Will the Israelis cross the Canal and enter the eastern bank? Or will they come from Suez?"

Mixed feelings surged within me as I walked on the terrace at my house in Giza. Without realizing it, I found I had been walking for two whole hours. I rushed again to the radio, but it was striking the same note: Our forces are in action. But no mention of the destruction of our planes. Once more I called Abdel Hakim. His reply was: "Al-Arish has fallen." This was the last time I spoke to him. The moment I put down the receiver, all was over between us. It was sunset on June 5, 1967. I called Gamal Abdel Nasser and said: "Gamal, go to headquarters and tell Abdel Hakim Amer to retire. You are the responsible commander-in-chief."

Night came and the Israelis started their psychological warfare; raids all night long over Cairo, the air-raid sirens never ceasing. My youngest daughter, Nana, was six years old at the time and was frightened every time she heard a gun or a rocket. I sent the children to the ground floor, then to Mit Abul-Kom, where I had built a home six or seven years before.

The night passed in Cairo, with anti-aircraft guns pounding, rockets firing, sirens sounding, and aircraft flying through the night until morning.

Silence struck me like a disease, and I believe it struck many. And here I stop to release a secret for the first time: I took the decision to launch the October War of 1973 just twenty-one days after the catastrophe of June 5, 1967. How this was carried out and why will be the subject of my next chapter.

Sadat's next chapter was never written. He was assassinated in Cairo the following day.

Abdel Hakim Amer was dismissed as commander-in-chief after the Egyptian defeat in June and committed suicide while under house arrest in September 1967. Sadat's official position at this time was Speaker of the Egyptian National Assembly.